Resonate

the stories we tell ourselves

BY CHRISTAL EARLE

May the words of this book remind you of how incredible your story can be.

Christal

Suite 300 - 990 Fort St
Victoria, BC, Canada, V8V 3K2
www.friesenpress.com

First Edition — 2014

Photography by Augusto Rosales

ISBN
978-1-4602-5401-1 (Hardcover)
978-1-4602-5402-8 (Paperback)
978-1-4602-5403-5 (eBook)

1. *Self-Help, General*

Distributed to the trade by The Ingram Book Company

Table of Contents

Part 1: Introduction

I used to have a crush on Jian Ghomeshi's voice. I used to love the way his sultry deep voice sounded when he would say great things like, "Canada", "radio", and "feelings".

He had many different guests on his show but one interview in particular rocked me to my core, and it was the most unlikely of people: J.K. Rowling.

She was doing an exclusive interview with him, talking about the release of her newest book at the time, *The Casual Vacancy*. She captivated me with her simple, almost shy approach to answering his questions. I loved that about her. She is *the* J.K. Rowling and she is trying carefully to find the right words for a radio interview!

Coincidentally, I had just finished reading the book the week before the interview. I loved it and felt that it was brilliant. It was so rich and full in its capacity to create a world of tangible characters that I fell in love with her writing all over again.

In Rowling's interview with Jian (aka, Señor Sexy Voice), she said something so profound, in response to a question that he posed. The question was around why she would bother continuing to write. It's not like she needed to, as she pretty much could put the success stamp on being the author of the Harry Potter series. But she hesitated for a moment.

She started and stopped.

Then she tried again.

"It's not really that I needed to write anything...Lightning doesn't strike twice. There was no way I could duplicate that kind of success...and when you have accepted that, that's great because now I feel very free to do what I want to do... One can become invested in your career being the most important thing in the world but it's simply not. "

She then went on to explain to Jian that in writing that book, she was reaching to the exploration of possibilities and of writing something that was completely from her.

That was how I felt when I first sat down to write this book, and it's how I feel about it now as I type this introduction. This book is not a "Potter" or any other claim to having arrived anywhere. This book is not a smoke show to make me feel like I have finally written something and got my name out there.

This is my gift to the person reading these words right now. Like J.K. Rowling, I have felt for a while that I needed to write something for myself, something for me to embrace as my own. But more than just a book for me, I hope that this work will also be for you, the reader, and that it will help you to consider your own story in life. This is me, sharing with you, how there is a path out of the confusion, the hurt, the colossal disappointment and the discombobulated mess your life can sometimes become without your permission.

And along the way, hilarity and heartbreak often go hand in hand.

I Could Have Sworn You Said Something Different

It's hard to describe the buzz that happens on a Hero Holiday trip. The air is alive with purpose, passion and awakening. It's like summer camp on steroids, life jacked up on Mountain Dew, and an emotional enema all rolled up in one. In short, it is amazing.

Hero Holiday is the name we dreamed up for a program we developed in 2004 in Live Different, the charity I helped to create and build. I was inspired to create something that would change the way we did things, and I believed these volunteer humanitarian relief trips for students had the potential to help change lives on a global scale--not only by helping others living in extreme poverty, but also by changing the perception of the students who took part in these trips. Part of Live Different's Hero Holiday experience is about helping to change the world, and allowing yourself to be changed in the process. The "Hero" part of the name came from recognizing the community members that work tirelessly, both in Canada and globally.

In 2007, I wanted to add something new to the experience. I dreamed of an internship program where we would invite returning students to apply for an extended month-long internship, working alongside our staff and volunteers and being immersed in an incredible personal growth opportunity.

It was a hit! The quality of the interns that joined us that summer in Dominican Republic far exceeded my wildest imagination and it had been one action-packed moment after another.

One day, we were about to head back to host a community celebration in the village where we had been working, building a school and community centre. It had become the place of many warm and life-changing memories and in many ways, as we had worked and supported each other along the journey, we had learned from each other and grown together in leaps and bounds.

That was something to celebrate, and I had a vision for how to add something extra to our community festivities that day. The kids in this community had nothing, at least nothing according to what we considered an acceptable standard of life. They were poor, and illiterate, and it had been that way for as long as anyone could remember. I wanted to do something extra special for them. In the spirit of Canadian summer memories, I wanted to create a bonfire complete with a lesson on how to roast marshmallows.

It would be the quintessential cross-cultural moment for our Canadian volunteers to teach the village children about an age-old campfire tradition from back home. I secretly congratulated myself on being so insightful and creative.

As I pulled into the parking lot of the grocery store with four interns and my translator, I hustled everyone into the building. My mission was simple: get in, get out.

I told everyone, "We just need to grab the marshmallows and get going, so that we get out to the site before the bus-loads of volunteers show up."

My translator, Bernard, was craving ice cream. Consequently, he ditched us for the ice cream freezer, leaving us standing alone over two bags of anemic looking marshmallows on the bottom shelf in the candy aisle.

This is never going to be enough, I thought. *We need more.*

As I was standing there with my interns, a store employee walked over and smiled at me. He began to speak to me in Spanish.

Problem number one: at this point, I knew only about 10 solid Spanish words and phrases.

I tried, through some creative sign language, to explain to him that we needed a lot more marshmallows. Did they have them?

He just smiled at me vacantly.

Enter worker number two.

Worker number two began to debate with worker number one.

Problem number two: I am getting frustrated that they are ignoring me and at the complete lack of any forward movement on the problem.

In total exasperation, I grabbed both their arms, and tried to explain "marshmallows" in the word that I thought they had used. I stood up tall and took a deep breath.

"Señors!" I began, with what I hoped was an authoritative voice. "I am about to have a grande fiesta and I just really want mucho, mucho *mamada*!"

Both men stopped and stared at me, their eyes wide.

Time was momentarily frozen. This was not the intended result I had hoped for.

My ears started to pulse, and my face grew hot. I had no idea what I had just said, but I felt panic rise inside of me. I tried to backtrack.

"Lo siento! I think I said something very bad."

One of the guys started to laugh, "No, señorita, you said something very good!"

First of all, I still didn't know what I had said, but I was quite sure I was going to regret whatever it was. Second of all, why didn't he let on earlier that he spoke English?

In confusion, I looked around at our little group that was standing there, and I saw that my translator had now joined us. And he looked shocked. Very shocked, actually.

"Bernard! What did I just say?"

The five seconds between my question and his response seemed like an eternity. Finally, he made one simple gesture. He put his ice cream cone back up to his mouth and pushed it in and out of his mouth with a sucking motion: the universal signal for what I just told the men I wanted to have in large quantities at my *grande fiesta*.

It definitely wasn't marshmallows.

In an effort to regain control of my last shred of dignity, I grabbed the two anemic bags of marshmallows from the shelf and started racing down the aisle, yelling over my shoulder at the interns, "Let's go, let's go!"

But it was a small grocery store, and by the time I reached the check-out counter (about three seconds) the whole store seemed to be in on what the crazy blonde chick had just announced in the candy aisle about her party.

It was a crash course in Spanish, and I learned words I hadn't ever considered needing to know! That story has become an urban legend in its own right, and many a volunteer who joined us for Hero Holiday has heard how *not* to ask for marshmallows at the grocery store!

Stories that are good never seem to die, do they? They stay with us. We forget the details but we never forget why we connected with that story.

For me, every time I meet someone who is learning a new language, I immediately relive that grocery store experience. It *was* hilarious, and it's now worth a good laugh, even at my own expense. My marshmallow story has given me compassion and admiration for others who are learning a new language. It's hard work, but there is a lot to be said for learning the language the right way and knowing how not to cause a ruckus in a local grocery store!

But I learned a lot from that experience, as well. I jumped to conclusions in our debate in the candy aisle and I had to pay the consequences. It also left me freaked out and intimidated to learn Spanish for a long time because I allowed it to make me feel inadequate and awkward. I took an experience and created an entire belief system around my abilities to speak a second language. A few random moments in life planted something much deeper in my perceptions of who I was and what I was capable of accomplishing.

It wasn't anybody else's issue, it was mine. It was a story I created around an experience that altered and inhibited my ability to embrace learning a second language. And it took a long time before I realized that the only person who had the power to change that story was me.

Why Resonance?

On January 13, 1990, the group Snap! released a song that became instantly recognizable all over the globe. It's called, "The Power." (As soon as I even typed those words, I could hear the high pitched, Aretha Franklin-esque voice cry out, "I've got the power!") It became a big favourite among fitness classes that were built on aerobics and step training.

And on that bizarre, fateful day, 21 years after its original release, on July 5, 2011, it shook up a 39-storey business center in Gwangjin-gu, Seoul, Korea.

Literally.

Imagine going to work, on a day that seems just like every other day. You pick up your morning tea, you stop to chat with the security guard, and you wave to friends across the hall. You sit down at your station, getting ready to focus on the day ahead of you and without warning, you start to feel like you are swaying back and forth. You think for a millisecond that it is just a weird vertigo moment, but as you look around you, you realize that everyone else is experiencing the same phenomenon.

Earthquake.

Like everyone else in that 39-storey building, you start screaming, "Earthquake!" and you take off for the nearest exit!

The rush down the stairwell is filled with frantic screams and desperate prayers. Everyone is focused on one thing: getting out of that building.

You finally reach the street level and come screaming out of the building, expecting the city to be alive with panic because of the earthquake. But slowly, along with everyone else who just poured out of the same building, you begin to realize that no one else in the city has noticed this earthquake. In fact, everyone else on the street is standing there and staring at everyone who just came streaming out of every possible exit in the building. Could it have been that your building was the epicentre of the whole event and it didn't affect anywhere else?

Kind of. But not really.

Because it wasn't an earthquake at all. It wasn't any kind of underground natural disaster, it wasn't wind, and it wasn't construction going on within the building. It was something far more powerful and surprising.

It was 23 fitness fanatics in a Taebo class within the mall on one of the bottom levels of the building, and they had no idea of the power that they possessed.

The zealous instructor had worked them into a sweat with the warm-up, and as they moved into the core of the workout when "The Power" blasted at full force, something happened that nobody could have predicted.

The fitness class stamped their feet and jumped in time to the music, oblivious to what was happening in the unseen realm of quirks, quarks and sound waves. As their feet and bodies created a subtle, almost imperceptible vibration in the floor, the inconceivable happened. The vibration that they were creating with their movements just happened to be at the exact same resonant frequency that was unique to that exact building.

Compared to the size of the building, their movements were ant-like, but when those movements, in a one-in-a-billion chance began to resonate with the building's unseen movements, all hell broke loose.

When the external vibration that was created by those 23 little passionate Taebo'ers hit the resonant frequency of the 39-storey building within which they were contained, the vibration amplified and caused the building to sway and shake so violently that it had to be evacuated for two days.

I bet that Snap! never saw that one coming. Neither did the rest of the world.

It's the power of resonance, and it's happening all around us all the time in every area of our lives.

What is Resonance?

In physics, resonance is the tendency of a system to oscillate or move rhythmically with greater power (amplitude) at some frequencies, more than others. Resonance surrounds us, but we are often unaware of it in the physical realm of energy and matter. It happens in all sorts of systems and situations and when two systems or things join up their frequencies, resonance can be as dramatic as an opera singer being able to shatter a glass with her powerful vibrato, or as destructive as bringing down powerful structures such as bridges and buildings. We know that everything is vibrating with energy (thank you, grade five science class). Vibrational energy is active outside of us and it's also alive inside of us. We can't help but be connected to it, and just because it is complex and beyond understanding for most of us, that doesn't mean it doesn't exist. Every day we hear the resonance of sound waves, feel the resonance of different movements, and trust the engineers who build the structures we live our lives in and around — unknowingly trusting that they have taken the resonant frequencies into account.

When something is resonating, whether it's a sound, a light wave, or energy particles, its strength is greater at some frequencies than others. Everything in our world is moving, seeking, searching to connect, and to continue to resonate on the same frequency as another object. When that happens—when one object connects with another and vibrates at a frequency close to the resonant frequency of another object—the movement, the vibration, gains strength.

I believe that just as resonance exists in the physical world, it also exists in our emotional, psychological and spiritual lives. We cannot separate them. We are complete beings, required to have all the necessary elements in place to function fully. How we each choose to define those elements may look very different and unique, but in the end, that choice is what makes us who we are.

When something we experience, hear or see "resonates" with us, it means that it will be made bigger through us, and that it will be more intense through that expansion. The experience has found a connection within us and, as it resonates, that connection gets deeper and stronger.

Each new encounter, experience or circumstance is an opportunity for resonance, for that encounter, experience or circumstance to resonate with us. Each of us has the power to choose how we will filter, act on, and process what we will focus on and what we will form our beliefs around. Emotions, history and default settings on our beliefs will all jockey for control of what will happen inside of us from that point forward.

Sometimes that choice is easier than at other times, and sometimes it's clouded by our resistance to growth and change. For many of us, there can even be times when we just plain and outright don't want to take responsibility for the choice because it seems easier to give in to the resistance and get swept up in the motion of what is happening than to take back control.

At the core of who we are is a choice. It's a choice that no one else can ever make for us, force on us or separate us from. Ultimately, it's even independent of our circumstances or limitations.

It's the decision to choose who we are, no matter what.

The Simplest of Lessons

It was beautiful in its simplicity. It had two round, upright wooden beams, held there by the flat beam that was nailed across the top of the two of them. Two ropes hanging down from that horizontal beam and a board between the knotted ends of the ropes completed it. It was painted white. It stood off to the side of our house, next to the Saskatoon berry bushes and just behind the teeter-totter.

It was where I learned what a "push" was, how to pump my legs back and forth to make it move more, and it was where I learned how to hold on tighter the next time to avoid a repeat of a painful face plant.

My legs weren't long enough to touch the ground yet, and my voice was probably kind of squeaky and giggly when I would call out to my dad to give me a push, whenever he got home after work. Somehow, that swing quietly worked its way into my childhood memories, reminding me that some things stay the same, no matter how old you become.

I learned many things on that swing about life and who I was. I learned about how far your wild imagination can carry you when you let it, giving you every reason to believe that someday you just might be capable of touching the sky on that swing. I learned not to sit on bees - or to tease them, for that matter. I learned that the wind carries different fragrances as it silently and invisibly whispers and dances around you. I learned that being a kid is a gift and I never imagined it would end.

There was something else I unknowingly absorbed during my time on that swing. Without any effort on my part, I gained an unseen understanding of what resonance was.

I have never taken a physics class in my life, but I have been operating in the realm of resonance since I was three feet tall. I just never knew it.

I watched and learned as my dad pushed me on the swing, and when my cousins would come over to visit, I mimicked what I remembered seeing him do. I would start them with one push, and wait as the pendulum end of the swing began to pull my cousin away from me in its arc. As it reached the length of its movement and began to swing back towards me, I waited for the perfect timing to give him a push, helping him gain momentum.

Even at the ripe age of four, I understood how to recognize the right time to give the push. You didn't stop it on its way up, and trying to make it move faster after it was already on its way down was pointless. The swing had its own idea of when it was ready to move back and forth.

You needed to catch it at the very peak of its oscillation and move with it, allowing it to determine its own momentum.

That swing was resonating, and its resonance carried me as I let the joy of the movement create greater space in me to dream and connect. The memory of that swing reminds me how good it feels to allow myself to resonate and flow with what is beautiful and effortless in life, no matter what it is.

That swing's lessons about resonance remind me that this life is a gift, no matter where I find myself.

But it's only a gift if I choose to see it as one.

You Are a Master Storyteller

Since the dawn of time, stories are how we have connected as a human race. They are how we have tried to make sense of everything, from the weather, to the seasons, to the differences between the sexes. Even now, in the 21st century, our world is filled daily with the stories that we recount, sometimes embellish, and always lean back on to communicate with each other.

But the mystery and beauty is that some of those stories seem to have more staying power than others. Perhaps it's because they resonate with us as they evoke a memory and we subjectively interpret it at will. It's the challenge of being human, isn't it? It's the insatiable need to take every event, every memory, every encounter, and organize it into one of two piles: good or bad.

But what if it wasn't good or bad? What if it just was? Perhaps actions and events, in and of themselves, are just neutral. Maybe it's how we choose to attach significance to them that gives them varying degrees of power.

Could it be that the stories we have chosen to believe about who we are, where we come from and what has happened along the way are not necessarily the full story?

So if this actually could be true, how would that change how you saw yourself? How would it change the inner conversation and chatter that is so active inside of your head for so much of the day?

Events happen, and as they transition to the past tense in our lives, they become the stories that we retell. They become history. As we look ahead of where we are, we tend to default to either anticipation or dread, judging the future from the present — or worse yet, the past.

Our systems of thinking and connecting are quick and imperceptible at times, but they are always on full alert. As someone shares their experience with us, at times we can experience a similar excitement / distaste / elation / disappointment to what they were sharing about. Like a radio frequency, we allow ourselves to tune into events, and that single, seemingly insignificant event resonates throughout our minds, giving us the illusion that it is confirming what we have experienced to be true.

Just like the power that resonance is capable of wielding in everything from bridges to swings to tall buildings, that same effect can begin to happen in us as we allow a message or belief to get stronger and stronger each time we encounter something that seems to enforce it. If that belief is negative and hurtful, it only continues to grow and take deeper root in us.

But it doesn't have to turn out that way. We can decide what we are going to allow to resonate in our beliefs about ourselves, our capabilities and our opportunities. The truth is that we are ultimately the ones that decide the stories that we are going to tell ourselves.

My story has grown to be about what I have chosen to tell myself and this is now my invitation to you to begin to do the same. The stories you are capable of telling yourself are worth the investment of time and the questions you are willing to ask about what you really believe about yourself.

Because you are worth it.

Does This Sound Familiar?

You can't sleep.

Again.

It haunts you as it forces you to spin things over, again and again in your mind. You run through scenarios, you make deals with the devil, you plead with God, you swear off candy, chocolate, bad movies and reckless shopping. You are determined that you are going to somehow, in some way, through some means of divine intervention figure this out.

And then, you can't.

You try again, believing that there has to be a way for it to release, there has to be a move of mercy that allows you to get to that point where it all becomes so clear. Yet, much to your frustration, that clarity eludes you, mocking you with its cloak of invisibility. You are left alone, yet again, without a hope of there ever being a way out of this whole thing. Somehow, some way, you have to believe that there is relief from it.

I mean, let's get honest here — for most of us, it's not like lives are hanging in the balance over our decisions. You are probably not the last bastion of sanity between two superpowers at the cusp of possible nuclear disaster. You are also probably not the last human to have contact with the psychopath standing out over the ledge, screaming at you to give her something to believe in or else she will jump. You are not even the last remaining special forces team member inside the cartel's compound, about to take down the global drug trade in one fell swoop.

You are just one little human, sitting up against the head board of your bed, staring straight ahead into the darkness so you won't obsess over the time on the clock on the table by your bed. You are going to need to figure this out.

Global history may not be hanging on your every move and your decisions aren't going to make or break the economy of some mid-sized country by 7 am — but somehow knowing that doesn't make it any better. Being aware of what you aren't a part of doesn't diminish the ache, the hurt, the utterly helpless feeling of being suspended in time, wishing you could have a do-over, wishing you had the opportunity to make it right, wishing you wouldn't have been so stupid, wishing they hadn't done what they did, wishing your pain could bring them back to life, wishing, wishing, wishing. Wishing that you could figure your way out of this mess and not feel like such a failure. Thinking back over the timeline of your life and wondering what is so wrong with you. How did everyone else seem to get their way and you somehow have been forced to choose between crappy option number one and crappy option number two. How did it get this far and how did it all get so out of control?

Perhaps those decisions aren't so little or insignificant after all. Perhaps those decisions are the ones that are about to change history.

But how will you know if you never get to that place in the middle of the night?

The truth is that I didn't start out thinking it would bring me to this place, either.

This is not where I thought I would end up – but then again, I don't actually know if I thought I would end up anywhere in particular. Perhaps I thought that I would just sail off into the sunset in a chariot of fire, never to be heard from again, escaping all the needless details.

But nope. No chariots here. No fire from the heavens. Not even a horse.

Only life and all of its twists, turns, momentary successes and seemingly colossal failures.

And if I was honest, I think I am kind of in awe at how much of life has caught me by surprise. Not in the, "Oh, hey there, life. I didn't expect that you would bring me a child or a divorce" kind of way.

No, this is in the, " I can't believe that you would grab me by the scruff of the neck, right when I was in the prime of getting my act together, chew me up, swallow me into an abyss and spit me out like it was my fault I was too distasteful for you."

Yeah, it was more like that, for sure.

Part 2: The Stories I Have Told Myself

CHAPTER 1:

JESUS AND THE FLANNEL-BOARD HORROR STORIES: STORIES OF FEAR

I remember the first time I encountered the fear. It was made of flannel and paper and it held my life in its hands.

I was five or six years old. I was playing outside and as the thought of eternity crossed my mind, I pressed the panic button. Eternity and all of its vagueness was not especially attractive to me at that moment.

I had been attending Vacation Bible School that summer and they were big on heaven and eternity and all those wonderful, ethereal concepts. (Those concepts still bend my mind even now, how did I ever process it back then?)

I remember a flannel graph board. It was dark blue and it transformed my world in one fell swoop.

My teacher that afternoon seemed so gentle. He really was a kind and loving man. At the time I thought he was ancient because he had grey hair, but in hindsight, he was probably only in his mid-thirties. He and his wife were a truly amazing couple. Each and every summer they would host little Vacation Bible Schools all over the outback of Saskatchewan, and those events were the highlight of my little six-year-old world. It was the best of both worlds for me: there were lots of kids, great music and hugs, cool snacks, and no schoolwork.

It was perfect. Until that day.

We were all sitting cross-legged on the floor, listening to our teacher kindly explain life, eternity and where it all came to a crossroads. He turned to the felt board as he talked, reaching into a clear plastic ziplock bag full of paper cutouts. Up on that felt board went pictures of nice little humans: boys and girls, old men and women, regular moms and dads. All of them smiling, clearly loving Jesus.

Okay, I am with you so far. I like pictures, I like my Mom and Dad, I like all of us getting along.

And then two more felt pictures went up on the board.

One of them was a felt cut-out of Jesus, standing on a cloud. He definitely wasn't the "Jesus is my Homeboy" poster Jesus. He didn't look goofy, he just seemed to be happy/sad Jesus and I was conflicted over how I even felt about someone who looked like everything about me and this sinful little life I was apparently leading made him look so sad. He had his arms stretched out, clearly waiting and wondering what was taking me so long to accept him.

In my mind I was trying to resolve these feelings. My internal dialogue went something like this: *Don't be sad, Jesus! I do love you, Jesus, I really, really, honestly, truly do love you. I think your clouds are fluffy and inviting and I think you are really awesome. I love you to the best capabilities of my little six-year-old heart.*

But while I was thinking this, trouble was stirring at the bottom of the felt board. All was not well and there was a disturbance brewing. Darkness, judgment and eternal pain were percolating in the southern regions of that little flannel board, and I never even saw it coming — I was too focused on fluffy clouds and happy/sad Jesus.

Unbeknownst to me, a second piece of felt went up and clung to the bottom of the board. And now, as I drew my attention towards it, I could see that it had flames of fire that licked up at the heels of the nice, benign looking multi-generational, Caucasian family. The flames of Hell were waiting to devour the whole family: dad with perfect hair, mom with apron, little Sammy in plaid shorts, and granny with hair bun and spectacles. The family was hanging on the precipice of destruction and had no idea. They were doomed! *That family better get their butts in gear, or they are done for*, I thought.

And that afternoon, in the middle of a country school in the outback of Saskatchewan, as I sat on the floor, spell-bound by the enormity of the drama that was playing out in front of me as that little felt family clung to the board, I was told of how we all had a choice to make in this world.

A choice?

What choice could we possibly have to worry about? We don't even know how to write full sentences yet!

But the choice was apparently quite cut and dry: there was heaven and there was hell. We had to choose either to love Jesus and accept him or to worry about the fire of Hell devouring our little sinful bodies in one raging inferno. Endless suffering. Pain. Separation.

"Who wants to accept Jesus?"

My hand shot up immediately. *I may not yet fully get what you are saying, sir, but clearly I don't want the alternative, so whatever you are selling, mister, I am buying!*

One quick prayer then and there, and it was crisis averted (whew). I was good to go. Upward bound. Heaven yes, hell no.

I left that little classroom that day not sure of what I had just decided to do, but ready to face the world on the other side. I was one of the good guys. I was on the winning team.

I had nothing but a bright future ahead of me. I had eternity figured out, so I was good to go. Or so it seemed.

However, later that afternoon, as I sat on my front porch, I began to recall something. It was something that I hadn't taken into consideration in the moment of passionate commitment as I negotiated my fire insurance policy.

We sat around that little flannel board and talked about hell being bad and heaven being good, but nowhere in there do I remember us talking about what we were going to do in heaven other than eat and sing. Now, as I sat there and thought things through, the only points I could remember about heaven (other than food and songs) was that I was told that I wouldn't know anyone in the same way. In fact, if my memory served me correctly, I remember the teacher telling us that we may not know each other in heaven, that our mom and dad won't be our mom and dad in heaven. That we all will be made new and we won't look the same.

And as that truth sank in, I pressed the big, red panic button of my little six-year-old heart.

There was nothing about that that was appealing to me at all! Why would I not want to know my parents? Why would I not want to look the same? Why would I want to go somewhere that I wouldn't recognize anyone and I would be alone? What if I didn't particularly like the food that they were serving up?

Now, I was the one caught between heaven and hell. I had buyer's remorse and I didn't know how to make it un-remorseful.

Fear kept me in a temporary conflict about the decision I'd made for eternity at six years old, but it also started what would become a lifelong battle with a fear far greater than I could ever foresee.

It set me up to wrestle with fear-based decisions.

And in case you are wondering, fear-based decisions never end well.

"Men go to far greater lengths to avoid what they fear than to obtain what they desire." ~ Dan Brown

What would you do if there were no limits?

Chances are, like me, you have been asked this question countless times. Perhaps, like me, you have brazenly answered it according to what you think will impress the listener or to what you have already decided is too big anyway, so you might as well shoot for the moon.

If I am being honest with myself, I like the idea of life without limits. I really do. However, I don't think that either you or I will experience that state of being in this lifetime. There will always be speed limits, universal laws of gravity, and some things that money - or MasterCard - cannot buy.

Limits exist. Deal with it.

But limits aren't really what we fear in the end; rather, we fear the open-ended possibility of limitless potential. Fear is about how I feel about myself. It's ultimately a control issue. If I decide I fear something, it helps to feel like I at least have control of something in my life. That fear gives me a sense of boundaries and measurable limits. I may not know how the freedom from something will feel, but I can easily grow comfortable in my pain and in the fear of not living without it.

The problem with fear is not in its existence; it's in its illusions of grandeur and all-consuming power. We live our lives dreading the worst, fearing that which we cannot see. The phone call, the disaster, the diagnosis, the abandonment, the failure, even the success. In short, we fear what we have determined to be unknown variables.

Fear has a tricky way of making us think that it's bigger than us. But no matter what story fear has told us about what's possible, it's never based on truth. If we truly want to write a different script for ourselves, truth is the only foundation that we can build upon.

The Great Pretender

Once upon a time there was a marriage between two young, vibrant humans. They were full of life, energy, vision and excitement. They were brimming with optimism and hope, convinced that they were going to change the world. Theirs wasn't a drive for power or money; it was a drive to change the world, to do something that would leave a mark on history and help make the world a better place. They wanted to create something together that would impact society and create social change. They instinctively knew that in order for it to survive they would need to enlist the help and insight of many people around them. So they did. People began to join them from all over the map, knowing that they wanted to help build something that would make a difference and that would help to leave a marked difference in the world as they knew it.

It was a good vision, and as it grew, so did the people around it. It continued to gain momentum, attracting more and more eyes, hearts and resources. It was fueled by a vision and that vision was an all-consuming vision. But after a while, something began to stir inside of one of them. When the cost seemed to be so great, and the payoff seemed, at times, to be too little, Christal (one of the two humans in this story) would ask herself those questions that she didn't really want to know the truth about in the first place:

Is this going to last?

Will we escape this next impending disaster? (At times they seemed to be never ending.)

If I stopped bringing value to this entity and vision we have created, will I still be valuable as an individual?

What is left of me — of us — if this was all to crumble and fall? We have put all of our eggs in one basket. What if we are missing something that is essential to our longevity and success?

I would journal and rip it up. I would send emails to myself and then delete them after I read them. I would militantly not allow my thoughts to veer towards the what-ifs, even though I had this underlying sense that a storm was brewing.

And then it happened.

He sat me down.

"I need to talk to you."

The cracks in the foundations began to tremble. My fear of the unknown became irrational.

"It's okay," I flippantly answered. "We will get through this. We are not going to quit. I am not a quitter."

But the floor was shaking under my feet.

And when the crack ripped my world apart, I think the final straw that created the most damage was the crash and destruction of the pedestal I had unfairly put him on. Through all of my actions, my words and my stubborn refusal to see what was really happening between us, I refused to let him come down off that pedestal.

He needed to stay there so that I could feel like I still had some thread of control left in my life. But no one deserves to be on a pedestal, no matter who they are. Human is as human does and, at times, humanity is painfully flawed.

At times, I could feel the fear rising in the back of my throat. The fear of losing what I was hanging on to with desperate, white knuckles. It would tighten like a clamp around my chest, making it hard to breathe. I would lay awake at night wondering what I had done to bring this on, wondering how I could ever find my way back to the life I had envisioned I wanted and felt I deserved. But still the peace I was clawing through the darkness to find seemed to elude me. I was that flannel-board family. The flames of destruction were licking at my carefully structured layers of protection.

I used my faith, I used my personal charm, I used whatever I could to fight off the fear of losing it all. I told myself that if I just worked harder at being a good, inspiring person, I would be able to keep it together. I sought out help in every nook and cranny of life that I could find. I tried to reason with him, I tried to do whatever I thought I needed to do in order to make our life together survive, but it wasn't enough. It never would have been enough.

I was backed into a corner and fear held me there for a long time. I felt the pressure of so many eyes on me, so many people depending on me to pull myself back together. My fear of total, systemic meltdown in my life took over my power to make decisions for myself.

There was only one way to start to get control back in my world. It was time to stop making fear-based decisions, and only I could decide to stop. It was time to start writing a new story for my own life once again.

On the day when we finally decided our marriage was over, we were standing on the beach outside of our apartment in Dominican Republic. Three years of pain and instability came to a head. There were so many bizarre, ridiculous and unbelievably painful events that had occurred in the time leading up to that final conversation that it was inevitable. This was it.

I don't advocate for divorce, nor do I advocate for staying in a situation that only continues to hurt you day after day. But life happens and it is never as clear cut as we assume it will be when we first start out on the journey.

Making that decision was about more than a destroyed relationship. It was about giving ourselves permission to think about what life could be like without the pain. The thing that kept me clinging to the pain longer than I needed to was the fear of trusting anything other than what I knew. I was stuck inside my experience, and I couldn't find the map to get out.

I had been scared, more than anything, of feeling like a failure, fearing the judgment of those who would never understand what it was to walk in my shoes. But I was holding on to an illusion.

I told myself that it was because I was scared of losing him. He was mine, wasn't he? We made a vow, didn't we? That was partly true, but my fear hid the bigger truth. The truth is that he was never really "mine" to have in the first place. Life isn't about manipulating people and relationships because you have a need for entitlement and ownership. Love is not self-seeking.

But fear is.

I could no more make him be "mine" than my mom could make me like eating liver when I was a kid. I would eat it, but I never truly wanted it, and inside I resented being forced to eat it.

He had to choose if he wanted to be mine and I had to do the same for him.

When we finally stood there, facing each other and making that choice, I was momentarily surprised at how the world seemed to continue to go on around me. I am not sure what I expected would happen but it felt like the best and most painful decision, and the biggest surprise of all was that the birds kept flying overhead, the waves kept rolling into the shore, and the sun didn't fall out of its place in the sky.

But by making a decision that I knew I had no choice but to make, something else unexpected happened inside of me. The fear was gone.

I couldn't fully recognize what was happening at the time, but it began to reveal itself to me in little shafts of light. Little glimmers of hope that this could be an end - or a beginning.

I began to realize how much I had let fear determine so many of my steps and decisions. I had become a control freak because I was scared to lose control. I had allowed fear to make so many decisions and jade so many relationships that for once, it truly and honestly felt like I had been gifted with a second chance to see how life could be lived without fear.

I had to re-learn how to walk again without the weight of fear clinging to my back and making my steps unsteady. At first I questioned whether I deserved to feel this good after something so seemingly bad. But I knew that I had to connect with the real "me" that was there all along - the me that wasn't controlled by fear and its minions in my mind.

And believe me, it felt good. It wasn't the "living the dream life" kind of good, but sometimes "good" just is, and that's enough to get us started on the road to recovery from fear.

That was where my story with fear began to change, and I will never look back. In fact, new stories began to take shape in my life; stories that were based on possibilities instead of the agonizing grip of fear. Every day that I am here is another chance to resonate with hope and possibility. And life doesn't play favorites -- it holds that same opportunity for all of us.

What is Fear?

Challenging circumstances and crises will always show up at different points in our lives. Fear can come on suddenly when we are faced with a physical threat, overtaking everything from our breathing and bodily functions to our impossibly fast decision-making processes. The fear we feel in those moments is in response to a perceived threat and our instinct pushes us to respond to that threat.

But fear is also the type of emotion that can lurk in the background of our life, content to hang out and wait for an opportune time to remind us that we are vulnerable and never fully in control of our circumstances. This aspect of fear is patient, but persistent, as it waits for its time to shine.

But like anything else in life, the more we understand it, the better equipped we are to navigate it. Fear is only an emotion, and emotions are parasitic in nature. They can't exist without a "host." Unfortunately for us, we are the only hosts that fear likes to hang out with. But if we look at fear as just an emotion, we allow ourselves the luxury of seeing fear for what it really is...

Fear is a very well-rounded emotion.

One of the ways I have come to terms with dealing with my fear is to approach it like I approach the disciplines of yoga and health in my life. In short, I need to work with what I've got. Some days I feel like I can take on the world because I feel so in tune with my body and what I need that I have the confidence to make the right decisions for my health and future.

And then there are "those" days. The ones where I have one hand shoving brownies in my mouth and the other hand clicking through WebMD, convinced I have a rare form of something that is going to destroy my future. I beat myself up for not doing something for my physical and mental health, while simultaneously refusing to get up out of the chair and take the simple step that would put me back in control of my wellbeing.

Why is it so easy to give in to fear? Because our fear can eat away at everything inside of us, telling us we are on our own in this one. It's more than fear on its own; it's the fear of being alone.

It gnaws at our ideas, creeping into our headspace. It pulls on our minds every time we tell ourselves that we are going to be strong enough to withstand it. It reminds us of all the disappointment, the rage, the bitter taste of gall in our mouths after the last disappointment. Oh, the havoc it will try to wreak!

Fear is powerful when given the space to accomplish its purposes. But in the end it is just an emotion, and emotions need someone to agree with them. Without that agreement, they are bound to the limitations of their nature. There are many times in our lives when we agree with the picture that fear tries to make us believe: fear of the future, fear of rejection, fear of failure, fear of success. When we choose to agree with fear and allow it to sidetrack our plans, our hope or our peace of mind we lose control of the story that we will live in. But there is a better way! We can choose what we will believe about fear and our relationship to it.

Fear is blindingly nimble!

As an emotion, it almost seems as if it is able to both project and remember at the same time. It's a primal response to any perceived threat that comes into our world and it can actually serve as a wake up call to what we need to be on guard for; what we need to remember for survival. However, it's also able to cause us to jump to conclusions that may seem logical in a moment where we feel threatened or unsure. We can even make our fear-based assumptions so quickly that we may not be able to separate what is real and what is imagined out of fear.

How many times has your fear run away with you, causing you to draw irrational conclusions that you convinced yourself were real?

Fear will push and pull on our focus, our emotional energy and our best of intentions. It revels in the chaos of confused emotions and it will set up shop there if we let it, reminding us of how we failed in the past and convincing us that the future only holds much of the same.

We can be held captive by fear's whispers and reminders that we are not good enough, not smart enough, not strong enough, not enough of whatever we need.

Does any of this sound familiar?

Fear is thrilled when others are blamed for its actions

You might recognize this little tactic of fear: the one where your back is against the wall for something that was said or done, and out of your fear of what you might lose if you are truthful, you pull out the weapon that fear hands you: blame.

I have been there. Have you? I have felt the fear of the repercussions for my actions. It starts when we are small children. Out of fear of being discovered for being naughty, we blame the dog, the teddy bear, our friends, even the adult who is calling us to account for our actions. We have an aversion to taking responsibility and that aversion is fear at work.

Like a classic bait-and-switch move, our fear can make us shift the focus so that we are not found out. We may do wrong things, but it doesn't mean that there is something inherently wrong with us. We don't need to be afraid to admit to our mistakes or lapses in behavior. But fear wants us to feel that the opposite is true.

If you have ever seen or fallen into the trap that fear sets through blame-casting, you probably also know that this particular tactic never ends well. In fact, when our fear leads us to blaming someone else for something we are too scared of being accountable for, that blame can cause a rift in our relationships and connections. It will often cause a divide that is hard to get past, unless we are willing to stop giving in to our fear.

Fear is incredibly seductive

Much of my own energy has been spent being courted by fear and listening to its seductive whispers.

I have had unreasonable fears, ones that are kind of humbling to put down here in black and white. It's not the fear of sharks or clowns that some of my friends truly have (even though the shark fearers often live on the prairies!) and it's not the fear of a natural disaster or of zombies. No, my fear is much more private, much more personal.

I wrestle with the fear of being found out.

Often, when I walk off a stage after giving a speech, with applause still ringing in my ears, when people tell me how much they are encouraged by me or how much they admire me and what I have done, I feel that same old fear threaten to come up and bite me in the butt.

It's the voice in my head, questioning whether I really deserve what I have, telling me that sooner or later, I will disappoint people, that I will somehow be exposed as not measuring up to whatever elusive standards I have imagined.

My fear found its strength in shame, and every time it would sneak up, I would allow the fear to resonate with the deeper parts of me that felt shame at who I was. It's the great Imposter Syndrome and I have been paralyzed more than once by it. Fear reasoned with me in my mind, seducing me to ease off on the pursuit of my purpose and calling in life, reminding me that I don't really deserve to be fulfilled and happy.

"But in the End, Fear is Just One of Many Emotions"
- Danielle Laporte, The Fire Starter Sessions

Because of fear's ability to be a shape shifter in our emotional lives, it can be difficult to be specific with it at times. It will mold itself to whatever situation suits it best as it tries to remain rooted in the decisions surrounding it. Disguised as anything from prudence to protection, the very ambiguity of fear's limits make it appear bigger to us than it really is.

Our emotions are real, but they aren't always the truth tellers in our lives. They make us feel alive, feel connected and can propel us forward, but in the end, we have the power to control them.

And no matter how much we may be tempted to believe it, it's never the other way around.

I Got Tired of that Story, So I Wrote a New One

The first time that I truly understood that fear was an emotion was when I decided to end my marriage. I had been scared of letting go of something that was no longer within my grasp anyways. Recognizing that fear was truly an emotion that I could control, and not a dynamic entity that could control me was an awakening. In many ways, it was like a re-birth of who I was meant to be all along. I was humbled and exhilarated by the truth as I began to understand it. I came to realize that, in the end, I was the one that gave fear its power.

Like many negative emotions, fear is exhausting, debilitating and frustrating. Fear will never help you gain perspective, it will never help you dream of a possible different outcome, and it will never give you permission to follow your heart. Fear doesn't like to give up control.

But when we finally get tired of fear's tactics, it's time to write a new story.

For me, it meant it was time to rebuild my life.

Rebuilding is harder than building something the first time, mostly because we have to clean up the mess left over from the other disaster. The freedom comes in choosing to let go of fear. When we do this, we allow our eyes to begin to focus on something that we have probably desired for a long time: clarity. As I learned to see fear for what it was, I soon found myself desiring the clarity more than just dodging the fear. Clarity actually began to feel so natural, like I was meant to have it all along.

And I think all of us truly deserve clarity about ourselves and our own lives, don't you?

Many times I have asked myself whether a life free from fear can possibly exist. I am not sure it can, to be honest. I am still scared of snakes, spiders and big waves on the ocean. I still have fleeting moments of being scared that things won't turn out the way I want them to or that I will fall flat on my face, yet again.

But I am learning to manage my fear and to recognize that it is just one of the emotions along for the ride — it's not sitting at the wheel. I have chosen to build the story of who I am around something much bigger than fear's limitations. And that story looks, feels and sounds a lot like how I imagined freedom to be.

What About You?

Are you one of the lucky ones who doesn't feel fear at making decisions you don't want to make, or didn't ever expect to have to make? Or has your story resonated so much with fear that it's hard to imagine how not to allow the fear to limit your willingness to dream, to make a decision and to take action?

Fear isn't static. The more you feed it, the more it grows. It can get rather insatiable at times, and we have to recognize it for what it is: a monster of our own making.

Does fear resonate in your story? In your relationships? In your understanding of who you are and what you are capable of? In your willingness to take a risk (not just sky-diving or bungy jumping — the real risks of loving, trusting, believing)?

Have you ever felt fear overflow into your judgments of others? Like trusting someone enough to get to know them better, even though they remind you of someone who hurt you or disappointed you in the past?

Have you ever asked yourself what you are really afraid of - and then asked yourself why you are so afraid in the first place?

When we acknowledge fear for what it is we are able to strip it of its power because we are not wondering what it looks like or how it will make us feel. It will always make us feel the uncertainty, the panic, and the threat to our security.

But once we feel it, recognize it and acknowledge it, we can also open the path in front of us to something far more beautiful and secure: clarity. That clarity is what is able to create space for confidence in our own ability to find the path again.

And, oddly enough, clarity is found in the willingness to ask more questions. Asking ourselves questions about what motivates us, and what is possible if we are willing to think differently and re-frame our stories, could be the very thing that frees us from the tyranny of fear.

Ultimately, freedom from fear, and the clarity that freedom brings, can help us decide what we want to move towards, rather than trying to figure out how to run away.

Don't be scared to trust yourself again, don't be scared to believe in trying one more time, and don't ever be scared of the hope of better days ahead.

In the end, it's the only story worth telling and remembering.

Chapter 2:

The Kool Aid Cop Chronicles: Stories of Death and Birth

Mile markers.

In 2008, I went backpacking in Turkey. It was an amazing experience full of great people, scenery, culture and hookah pipes filled with apple-flavored air. But if I was to be honest about it, I am not a hard-core backpacker. I have come to realize that when given the chance to choose between adventure and shopping, I will create a new category: adventure shopping. My penchant for finding treasures always seems like such a great idea until I have to hoist said treasures onto my back and walk around a massive cosmopolitan city in search of a cheap hostel – mostly because I blew the travel budget at the market.

However, adventure shopping aside, Turkey is a wonder to behold. I was especially excited to visit Ephesus to walk the same ancient stone streets as people I have admired and studied. I thought I would feel this sudden thrill of connection with ancient history that would change me forever, like a cross between an Indiana Jones movie and an old-school BBC documentary that marveled at the mysteries of the ancient world.

However, the ruins of Ephesus are filled with tourists from all over the world, just like me, and it can be hard to actually get in the zone of ancient thoughts with everyone frantically snapping photos all around you and posing on ancient toilet seats.

When we finally reached the massive ruins of the 24,000-seat theatre, I sat in one of the seats and wondered how it would have felt to be a condemned prisoner or enemy of the state and have my death become a spectacle in that same theatre in front of a taunting crowd. I wondered who had sat there so long ago, what their lives were like, and how they connected to the world around them. I savored every minute of it, imagining the history in that exact spot on earth.

Later that afternoon we walked along the road outside the city and I began to notice ancient mile markers. Indicating distances and directions to the next town, they had Roman numerals on them and the name of the king or ruler from that ancient time. My 21st[t] Century sandaled feet walked on a road that streams of humanity have used for countless years. Each person along that road had been the owner of ideas, dreams, plans, hopes and fears, just like me. Some of them would have entered and left the ancient city as free citizens, some as slaves; some might have been rich, others devastatingly poor. Each new mile marker that they passed by contained vital information about where they were and which direction they headed. I wondered what they thought and felt in those moments. Did they have any sense of connection to their experience, to their fellow travellers, or to the world that surrounded them? Did they feel anticipation or dread when they saw those mile markers?

And the truth is that thousands of years later, mile markers still happen in our lives today. Sometimes, whether we recognize it or not, they are capable of defining our lives, our stories and our future.

One of mine was a Phone Call

Sometimes it seems like it was so long ago.

Sometimes it seems like it was yesterday, and I am standing in that hallway in my house, tearing through a pile of photographs, panicked that I will forget what he looked like, forget what his voice sounded like, forget his laugh, his smile, his walk — panicked that I will forget how his hands looked.

I had just hung up the phone. I was in the living room. I stumbled into the hallway, reaching out into the air, trying to grab onto something that wasn't there -- gasping, crying, screaming, while I felt the rush of a vacuum of loss.

Time and eternity had just had a cataclysmic collision and I was left in the aftermath.

I ran down the hallway of our house, trying to find something, anything, to remind me of Andrew. Anything that could make it not real, that could make it less painful.

It couldn't be true. He was very much alive in my mind and in my memory. My brother was too young, too full of life, too full of promise, too much alive to be dead.

Pain gripped my ribcage, threatening to crush my lungs. Was I breathing? Was I even awake? Was this a dream? What was real, what was the nightmare? As my arms flailed about me, I grabbed a picture off the shelf. It was of the two of us, sitting on a park bench together. We looked so young. So unconcerned. So alive.

When we were little, I remember sitting on an open, flat trailer, behind a tractor (yep, I grew up on a farm in the middle of Saskatchewan). My dad was taking us out with him to do chores. We needed to get some square bales of hay to feed the cows. As he backed up the tractor towards the pile of bales, I remember having simultaneous thoughts.

The first was that the way the bales were stacked made them look just like Shredded Wheat (a breakfast staple in my family) and it made me feel hungry. The second thought was about what he had just told me before he started backing up the trailer towards the pile of bales: to keep an eye on Andrew. At the time, he was too little to know how to be careful for himself and my dad wanted me to hold my little brother's hand to keep him in place.

We started to back up. I started to think again about breakfast cereals and how good they would taste just then. Our trailer was now backed up to a 15-foot tall pile of straw bales. Dad reached for the kill switch to turn off the tractor. But as he went to step off, the clutch jumped the tractor back, lurching it against the pile of bales. The rest was a slow-motion episode from a dramatic Disney movie scene.

The pile of bales started to quiver and as time stood still, one started to sway, causing the ones beside it to do the same. They swayed further and further, back and forth, back and forth. I was mesmerized by the giant Shredded Wheats that were bending and swaying, high above us -- even as they started to fall over.

Directly down on top of Andrew and me.

They didn't feel like light and fluffy breakfast cereal when they crashed down.

I remember thinking, in my little, valiant six-year-old brain, that I needed to protect Andrew. I threw myself on top of him as the bales started to fall onto our trailer. One or two hit against me and knocked me off balance, throwing me off of Andrew. They subsequently knocked the wind out of my lungs, as well.

Dad jumped on the trailer and grabbed us both, clearing us out of harm's way, as I kept sucking for air, trying to recover from the shock of being assaulted by life-sized Shredded Wheat. He held me and told me to stay calm, reassuring me that my breath would come back if I stayed calm.

He was right. But getting my breath back also gave me the power to begin to wail and sob, in terror from what had just happened. Thinking, most of all, that I had failed to keep Andrew safe. I couldn't change what had just happened. I had no control. Through no fault of my own, I felt like I had failed at what I was supposed to do.

To this day, I feel as if I can remember every moment of that accident. It's a mile marker — a story of feeling like I didn't do a good enough job at a simple task: to protect someone I loved and create the assurance that they knew how much they meant to me.

That afternoon, as I stood paralyzed by shock in the hallway of my home, I could see that whole incident play out again in my memory. I was weak and incapable of stopping something that wanted to destroy my world. Like an insatiable beast that relentlessly preyed on the corners of my security, the feeling came back to me in an instant: the feeling of not being enough. And oddly enough, all of my life, I have wrestled with how to tell myself a different story.

Hey, Kool Aid Man!

Long before the world knew that there would be an internet, social media or electronic devices beginning with the letter "i," there was an iconic figure. He ruled the world in a time called the '70s and '80s, when people actually sat through commercials on their favorite television shows. In my imagination, he was the hero to children all over the world, and he always came when they called out to him by declaring how thirsty they were on a hot day.

He was the Kool-Aid Man. He had his own theme song, he wore great long socks and shoes, and he always, always busted through brick walls, to rescue thirsty, urban-dwelling children playing basketball in a nameless concrete park.

Man, did I ever want to be one of those kids. They were living my dream. They were in a city, they were on TV and they were famous.

Instead of living in a city and being famous, I lived on a farm in Saskatchewan and had to entertain myself with invisible friends because there were no other kids to play with other than Andrew, my younger brother. And clearly, he didn't count, according to how I surmised the situation.

But the solace that my mom offered me was the next best thing: we diligently saved our UPC symbols from Kool-Aid packages and mailed them off in a self-addressed, stamped envelope to the elusive Kool-Aid Man who lived in a far-off city I dreamed of at night.

Four to six weeks later, as promised in the advertisements, two shiny, new plastic cups showed up in the mailbox at the end of our long, country driveway. They were miniature cups shaped like the Kool-Aid Man - one red, one blue. Kool-Aid tasted so much better, so much more real, just by being inside of those cups! They were practically like a rare china pattern to me. I loved them and loved to drink out of them. I vowed that for the rest of my life I would drink my Kool-Aid only out of those cherished vessels.

As my mom would pour Kool-Aid into them on a hot, long summer day, I would stand vigil over the process, making sure that there were exactly equal amounts in both cups. I was just tall enough to see over the kitchen counter, so I was in the perfect position to stand guard. I was militant and on a mission. There would be nothing but equality in this home. Especially when it concerned me.

I was the self-appointed, self-regulated, self-exalted Kool-Aid Cop, and I was darn good at what I did. In fact, I was the fairness cop in every area of life. I obsessed over making sure that Andrew never got more than me, that I always felt like the treatment was fair, and that there was never even a hint of anyone being treated with favor over me. The reasons for my obsession with equality eventually became clearer to me as I learned to process many hard-earned life lessons. It was about an old belief I held tightly to for many, many years, thinking that I was the only person who ever struggled with it. The belief that I am not enough.

I couldn't be as good as I wanted to be, no matter how hard I tried. I couldn't ever be a good enough daughter, sister, friend, or team mate. I wasn't pretty enough, I wasn't quite cool enough, I wasn't good enough. I truly felt that I was not enough, even though, to this day, I am still not sure what "enough" really is.

Somehow, somewhere along the line, I began to believe a lie about who I was, what I was capable of, and what I was going to have to do in order to be someone that mattered.

For many of us, the sense of not being enough can come into our story from early on in life. All too soon we begin to notice the differences between us and those we wish we could be more like. We compare and contrast, wishing we had what they had. Our hyper-sensitive antennae are on high alert for any signals we might pick up about our worth and where we belong in this world. Every word, action, error and omission can play into how the story takes on shape and form.

Until one day we wake up and don't realize how the story strayed so far from the truth.

And then, the Phone Call came...

For some strange reason, I found myself standing in my hallway that Friday morning, clinging to a picture of my brother and me. Teardrops fell onto the glass inside the frame, as I ached to be able to hear Andrew's voice one more time. I was so scared I would forget what it sounded like. The world would never again hear his laugh or see his smile. How would I ever be able to recall it when I needed it most?

I had no sense of an ending and, because of that, was not able to grasp fully that he was really gone.

Later on that night I stood beside his body, in a cold, starkly white hospital room. The sterile environment was foreign and painfully devoid of compassion for our little family who stood around his body, laid out on that hospital gurney. There was no way he could be dead. I kept repeating a wordless mantra of disbelief to myself, hoping to change it all somehow. Wishing for a miracle of epic proportions that would raise him from the dead and remind the world that miracles still happen if you only have the faith to believe.

I could have sworn I saw his chest move, just the tiniest amount. I held my breath. This could be the miracle moment...

But he didn't move. And as I stood there, wrestling with accepting the fact that he was truly gone, I remember thinking about the stubble on his face, and how his hair still looked perfectly done. Surely this wasn't how someone looked when they were dead? Surely this can't be happening.

But it was happening.

In fact, it already had happened. I just needed to accept the fact and move forward with life from this point.

That moment, in that room, became a defining moment for me. I accepted something that I had no control over. Andrew was gone and, looking at my parents across the room, I came to the miserable conclusion that not only was I the one that was left. I was *all* they had left.

WHAT IT CAN BECOME

Andrew died in a workplace accident. He was 20 years old. He was my brother, my friend and my nemesis, all rolled up into one, all of our lives. We were worlds apart and yet so much alike. I was demanding, he was stubborn. I was bossy, he was mischievous. I was always challenging whatever my parents said, he was always the one that figured out a way to just get things done. I tried everything out to see if I would like it. He just kept quietly pushing on, allowing things to reveal themselves to him in due process. I was always on the go, he was relaxed.

Everyone has a story to tell about their childhood, their relationships, their family issues and their conclusions.

I am no different.

But the story that I told myself after Andrew's death became a much bigger story than my own. It became about taking what I had experienced and turning it into something that was useful, inspiring, captivating and consuming. The story of his death and how it affected me became one of healing and transformation, and one of blood, sweat and tears.

It was a story about what a vision is capable of becoming: the good, the bad, and the less than desirable. That vision for Live Different consumed me, sustained me and carried me to places and experiences I would never have dreamed of. It made me who I am today and helped to shape where I am continuing to travel on this journey.

But it had to start somewhere and it started that night, standing in that white hospital room, as I let my tears fall onto my brother's immovable chest that covered lungs that no longer needed air.

Four nights later, as I sat on the floor in his bedroom, I could still smell him. I imagined him sitting there, only a few short days before, and I tried to evoke the sound of his voice, his laughter, his presence in that room with me. I spotted a Bible on the bedside table. It was a gift I had given him two years earlier, as he moved away from home for the first time. As I thumbed through it, I found that it had one verse underlined in it. Jeremiah 29:11.

> *I know the plans I have for you, says the Lord. Plans to prosper you and not harm you. Plans to give you a future and a hope.*

I thought about all I had lost, all that Andrew had lost, all that never was. I thought about what many of us have probably wondered from time to time in life as well.

I thought about how there had to be more to life than this. There had to be something greater, something that I was capable of doing, of becoming. I wanted to believe that I had the potential of building a legacy for the future. I wanted more and I wanted to be able to do more meaningful things.

I dreamed of making my life count for so much more, of helping to change lives and bring hope. I could see it coming to pass, in my mind's eye, and I could almost reach out and touch it. Sitting on the cold floor in my brother's now empty room, the seed of a vision was planted inside me, and I was determined that I would see it come to fruition.

Sometimes a life vision happens like that, and even though you don't know how you are going to make sense of it at the time, you know that whatever "it" is, it's going to happen. And once you are at that point, it becomes nearly impossible to be convinced otherwise.

Come hell or high water, you are going to see it come to pass.

It starts as a seed

A seed isn't much to look at. It's often puny and dried up and seems to resemble almost nothing of the potential for life that it holds deep inside. Its future is not visible to the naked eye at the time, and it's not that impressive – unless you see it through the eyes of what it's capable of becoming.

The beautiful, unpredictable, strong and limitless possibilities of what that seed contains will come to pass if given the right conditions. But like anything worth growing, it might take a lot of hell to get there.

It might have to push against hard, angry ground, believing it's moving towards the light and the source of its survival. It's the only way that little seed is able to make the journey that it will undertake to become the fullest expression of what it's intended to become. It contains everything it needs to make it happen, but not even the seed itself may know that at the time.

We all hold the power to choose to resonate more with the hope of the seed rather than the loss of the tree. Life, hope and future is found in the seed. The seed is going to undergo many changes in the days ahead, but all of those changes are pushing it towards the ability to reach its potential.

When we decide to start to change the story that we are resonating with, the first steps can always feel awkward and painful. As we stretch to find a new rhythm to fall into with our thinking and actions, we can have great successes and devastating failures. The cycles of emotions can threaten to roll over you at any time, un-welcomed and uninvited. The anger, the disbelief, the anger again, the hopelessness, the anger again, the emptiness, and eventually, without even realizing it, the acceptance comes in and begins to open your eyes and your heart to the future. And the future is always open to persuasion because it's still waiting to be formed. To a great degree, it's dependent on our choosing, and we steer towards whatever we are focused on.

The seed inside of me was the seed of deciding what I would believe about who I was. It wasn't positive self-talk or "naming it and claiming it" that made the difference. It was a basic, elementary choice that I decided I would make over and over again, for the rest of my life.

On the day my brother died, I chose to believe that I *was* enough and I *was* capable of doing incredible things – even though I didn't feel it or connect with it at first. Feelings are secondary when it comes to our decisions around our beliefs. The feelings, convictions, and assurances eventually come but, as with any change, there needs to be an adjustment period, a time when you allow yourself to feel out the new space you are moving into.

Almost daily I would begin to notice that I had the *choice* to believe in my "enough-ness" or not. The power of that decision had been mine all along, but I had never had the courage to ask myself the bigger questions that had plagued me for so long. Questions such as what my gifts and talents really were, if I really mattered and if I would ever be capable of living in freedom from the insecurities that had plagued me for so long.

In the end, those questions weren't even that scary. I had feared what I didn't understand or recognize, purely because it was an unfamiliar space to me.

And like a brand new home waiting for the new owner's funky, classy and personal touches, that space is being held for each of us. That space is patiently waiting for the day when you will make a statement to the world of who you truly are.

That seed of choice and belief has the same potential for all of us. Believing and feeling are not always on the same page inside of us, but when they are going in the same direction, they eventually begin to start to walk side by side.

Agreement is an incredibly powerful force to be reckoned with because there is strength in numbers.

So what are you going to choose to agree with?

One Day I Lifted My Head Up

Starting Live Different was a birth that followed death, my brother's death; and like every life that is birthed, it changed me. To a great degree it even sucked life from me in the early days, as I worked with a tireless group of people just to keep it alive.

And in an inexplicable way, it made me wish I could do it all over again. It was a vision that was so big and so passionate that it was able to take on a life of its own. It started one year after Andrew's death, and it began with my husband and I selling everything we owned, giving away the rest, packing our world into a 1975 Volkswagen van (I can't even remember why on earth we chose that vehicle) and moving across the country.

The beginnings were anything but pretty or glamorous. We had nothing but a big dream, a lot of debt, and the guts to hang on because we didn't have a plan B. We lived in an

80-year-old lady's basement, did our dishes in a laundry tub, cooked in a toaster oven and on a George Foreman grill. We shared the space with people sometimes sleeping under the table because there was no second bedroom. Our landlady was certifiably senile and would wander around naked, leave burners on and didn't seem to think it was a big deal when her crazy cat peed in our shoes, on our bed or in the middle of anything we owned.

We started doing whatever we could: living a lot on the road, traveling as a band and presentation group, shaping and forming the dream of getting in to high schools and creating something that had never been seen before. Some days we nailed it, other days we were terrible. But every day we knew that we were a part of something so unique and life-giving that we needed to hang on and believe in what it could become.

People came from all over to join us throughout those early years. Every time I stood on a stage, in a classroom, or was present in a conversation or moment that was illuminating and hopeful for someone else, I was reminded of why I had chosen this vision - or maybe why it chose me (I don't know if there is really a difference anyway). Sometimes I felt as if I was vibrating from all the energy and excitement of being a part of something that was making a difference.

But, I had also given my entire life, energy and resources into the survival of this fledgling organization. I was propelled and compelled by the deep, driving passion to continue to grow this vision, to continue to do what hadn't been done before, and to change lives in the process. We were building a whole new model for how to create personal and global change, and while it was always exciting, it was also ceaselessly demanding. We were continually touring across the continent doing motivational presentations throughout the school year and leading humanitarian trips in the summertime with hundreds of volunteers. Even though it was always exciting and evolving, it was a grueling and exhausting pace to maintain. I ate, breathed and dreamed about all that could be done through this vision of seeing lives changed by the purpose and hope that comes when people realize the power they have to make a difference in the world and the results that come from having a hands on experience in humanitarian work.

One day, I lifted my head up from working so intensely for so long and I looked around at all that was going on. I was amazed at what I saw happening. Like watching a child grow and mature, becoming more confident and sure, I saw that we had grown far beyond what I had ever dreamed possible, and it had happened without me even realizing it.

All I felt was awe. Life-changing, humbling, awe. One person doing great things is commendable, but there is something uniquely powerful when people work together for a vision bigger than themselves. We come alive when we live our passions, gifts and talents out on a bigger scale, allowing ourselves the opportunity to fill a space that makes the whole picture beautiful. This unwavering belief in our vision is what came to be the heartbeat of our entire organization.

We were definitely not perfect. In fact, we were very far from the ideal of how a start-up should happen. We had more nerve than wisdom and more zeal than the ability to follow through with it all. Along the way, there were too many failures and near-misses to count. But the successes made it all worthwhile. We succeeded in more ways than I was even initially willing to acknowledge. I can be both humble and confident enough to say that we accomplished some amazing things since our inception and I am forever proud of those accomplishments. I have witnessed lives being changed through the projects we have built around the world: we have helped to change the stories of individuals, families and communities and I will never, ever regret a moment of it.

All in all, I don't know if I would change this new story that I wrote for myself. It is the story of how a devastating death became a story that resonated with life. And that life has become very beautiful in its own unique way.

Everything we do, say and choose in this life has far-reaching effects. Backseat babies are conceived from a momentary lapse in judgment. Democratic global leaders rise and fall according to individual votes and choices. Childhood is marked by scars or successes based on simple words and actions of influential voices at key moments in our development.

And through it all, we are consciously and unconsciously constructing the stories we believe. We create, build and frame our views of who we are on these experiences. We tend to find comfort in processing our life experiences as either good or bad, right or wrong, black or white. Perhaps by doing this, we feel that we are somehow in control of our lives and in where we are going. It's our default switch for processing and it's really hard to trip the switch. But hard and impossible are in separate worlds, aren't they?

Control isn't about "being in control" of something or someone. Control is about the choice we make about who we are going to be and what we will find our value and meaning in.

We affect where we are going and how our lives will influence the future with every single choice we make. From the moment we get up each day, we are making influential decisions about everything from our physical and mental health, to the future of our relationships with each choice we make along the way.

And those choices, those words, those actions, those stories that we choose to believe about what makes us who we are hold something far more powerful than we could ever imagine. Ultimately, they hold resonance.

In my brother's death, I found life. Call it cliché, call it cheesy, call it whatever you want. But I will call it one of the stories that I tell myself about my life and my future. It's a story that ultimately created confidence in me to hang on and believe that there was more.

Because there is always more if we are willing to look for it. The universe we are a part of is always expanding and creating space. Growth keeps us on a forward, ever-expanding continuum and it doesn't ask for our permission to do so. We are a part of that expansion and we have all the space we need to fulfill those deeper callings and desires for significance.

If that's part of the world we inhabit in the here and now, should we be surprised when we find hope and growth the moment we let go of limiting beliefs about who we are and where we are going?

I vote with a resounding NO.

What We Have in Common

I used to find it easier to hide behind numbers. If I could count it or regurgitate it back as a form of knowledge, I somehow felt a sense of understanding and insight. But losing Andrew has taught me, more than anything else, that life is not about numbers. Our world finds and connects its meaning through stories. Those stories are about people like you and me. And we write them ourselves. We struggle, we overcome, and with each new opportunity and experience, we live our lives and decide who we are going to be.

Loss comes in endless forms. It's not just about death, relationship wrecks, or our physical state. It's about the ebb and flow of all that we are in this world.

Every loss makes way for a new opportunity, if we are willing to consider what that could look like.

As a parent, I feel a sense of loss every time my daughter needs a bigger size of shoes or reminds me that she doesn't need me to do something for her anymore. In my heart I want to celebrate with her, but part of me feels ripped off at the relentless passage of time. Yet, she is growing and as I focus on helping to make a place for her in the world, I grow with her in some beautiful, heart-shattering way.

Life is a long thread, and we choose how we will weave it. Its evolution comes about in our choosing and no one can do that for us.

We decide the stories we are going to tell ourselves.
Every. Single. One.

I bet you didn't realize how powerful you really are, did you?

Chapter 3:

Shiny Objects and Stories That Provide Us With a Go-Around

We were in Barbados. There was a group of us from Live Different, probably twelve in all. We were there to work with some local groups in schools and communities. I loved every minute of it and was grateful for the experience.

Our team was housed in a dorm-like facility on a large property in the town of Oistins. Every morning, in order to make our schedule run more smoothly, we would all help share the responsibility of making breakfast and preparing lunches for our day. At the end of each day, we would confirm that we had enough for making the meals the next morning.

And every morning, we would find ourselves confused as we tried to figure out how items were disappearing out of a locked kitchen, with only one window that was left slightly open, high up on the third floor. We would continually question the team, asking if anyone took the bananas and a few of the items that were left on the counter. No one owned up to anything.

This went on for five days, with no answers. I was getting ticked off. Surely someone wasn't 'fessing up.

But day five changed everything. There was a thief, and the thief got busted.

It was early in the morning. We were preparing another meal and heard a little muffled sound from the open doorway on the backside of the kitchen. Standing there, with a compact mirror in his hand that he had just swiped off the counter, was a bold-faced and defiant little monkey. As he stood there staring us down, he brazenly scratched his belly, daring us to come after him.

As he turned around and bounded down the stairs, we started laughing and took off after him. The whole team gathered around a massive tree behind the house, laughing and trying to coax the monkey to give back what he had stolen.

Mr. Monkey stood on the branch, with his back to us, looking at us over his shoulder via the mirror in the compact. He stared and stared, loving the inquisitive face that was staring back at him from the reflective surface. He was Narcissus and there was no way we were rescuing that mirror out of his clutches. He was lost in the beauty of the shiny object, and getting his attention was a lost cause.

I would like to be able to say that I have nothing in common with that monkey, but I would only be fooling myself. To say that I have never been mesmerized by shiny objects that came across my path would be a boldfaced lie.

The truth is that I heart shiny objects. I am especially in love with shiny ideas. New ones, big ones, little ones. I have no shortage of them, for myself or other people. They energize and excite me, and they can cause me to lose sleep in the anticipation of what they can become. I thrive on getting people excited about a vision and in helping them discover their significance.

Shiny objects can be so much fun! When they help other people find something that they didn't see before, they can be transformative. As they change the line of sight and help rekindle something that may have been lost along the way, they are helpful and can light the path in front of us.

But they can also be destructive. When we are tired of trying, or staying the course, it can be easier to just tap out and pursue something new, something more exciting and sexy.

These figurative shiny objects can appear as something designed to draw our attention in a new way. They can come along right at the point when we need to stay focused, right when we feel exhausted by hanging on and by trying and failing. They can seem like a way out of dealing with the task or issue at hand.

How can we not be excited by them? They hold the promise of possibility and sometimes they are just too enticing to ignore.

Like my little primate nemesis in Barbados, I have sought out way too many shiny objects. There have been many times when the need to be decisive and commit to something has left me frozen with the anxiety of indecision. It has felt like I am standing at a barren crossroads, with conflicting signs pointing to opposite directions, all of them urging me to follow their lead and go with their suggestions.

In those moments, instead of feeling like I have an inclination in one way or the other, all that is real to me is the rise of panic in my throat, and as the fight or flight instinct kicks in, I only want to choose flight.

And just when I need it the most (or, truthfully, the least)....tada!...the shiny object comes out of nowhere and inspires me to pursue something totally different. It's so much more alluring to go for something new and sparkly than to attempt to buff and shine up the old, worn out "stuff" in our lives.

Yep, I am way more of a lover than a fighter. A lover of new ideas and avoidance tactics, to be more precise.

When things became progressively worse in my marriage, I created a coping mechanism that became a crutch and a hiding place for avoiding what was really happening. It took a long time to recognize it because it wasn't something that could be categorized as bad or destructive — from the outside. Actually, it made me feel self-satisfied, and I began to take a perverse pride in my new pet, whom we shall name, "Go Around." Clearly I needed to take my eyes off of my own problems because they were just too painful to address on my own. And what better way to get my eyes off my problems than to hide in plain sight? Go Around and I began to look for ways to do bigger and better things in an effort to take the pressure off of dealing with what was happening in the present in the most foundational relationship in my life: my marriage.

I was going to fix my marriage from the outside. I was going to make him love me because of all the great things I did and I was going to prove to him, to myself and to the world how much I was worth the investment and how much value I added to everything. I think I actually had myself convinced that although there was clearly no precedent for this approach being successful in the generations of humans that had come before me, I would be the one who would prove that it was a successful tactic for avoiding pain and problems in my own little private world.

Instead of asking what I could do to clean up the mess in front of me, and to confront my fears head on, I just kept dreaming bigger. You should have seen the ideas that I came up with! I was on fire! I had more ideas and vision in that time than I knew what to do with. I dreamed up new businesses to start, new territory to cover in Live Different and, best of all, the new me that I was going to begin sculpting. That new me was so shiny, so full of inspiration and attraction that it was going to be revolutionary. The new me was going to be what would save my marriage, put my life back right-side-up and save the day - all in one fell swoop.

My ideas were really great (of course they were!). They were altruistic (mostly), they were for the betterment of humanity and, best of all, they were bound to be so successful that I could just point to them to remind myself that all was not lost in my world.

But here's the bite: I had erroneously convinced myself that there would be a way, someday, that the good would outweigh the bad, somehow. Surely God would take all those things into account and would pull through on what I really wanted - to have my world be whole again and to stop the pain and destruction that was happening in my private world.

It seemed like the perfect plan in my own eyes, so I just kept with it and talked myself into all the reasons it was going to be a surefire success. But He didn't do what I wanted Him to do. And that really, truly ticked me off.

What was there not to love about what I was doing? How could the Creator of the universe somehow miss the plain truth about how much I had sacrificed, how much I was doing for the greater good of humanity? Had He failed to notice all the crap I put up with that no one knew about? Had it escaped His notice that I had kept a lot of pain to myself, that I had covered up or compensated for other people more times than not, that I had silently (although not without resentment) kept on dreaming of new ways to advance the cause of good and just set aside my own problems and pain?

All of this, of course, was done in my martyr-like pursuit to help heal the world so how could it be that I wasn't getting what I wanted and needed? What the heck more could I do to get His attention? How many more flares did I need to send up to make Him realize that I was worth the investment of healing my pain?

And all the while, in the back of my mind, gnawing away at the core of who I was, lived the most destructive pain of all: the unanswerable question of whether I was worth it in the first place.

And the longer I waited and the less likely it seemed that the lifeboat would appear, I came to a conclusion: I must have either done something to bring all this pain on, or worse, had not been worth the effort of healing in the first place.

Sound ridiculous? It sure does. Until those are the shoes you are wearing, and all of your world, your values and your future comes into question. And although you want to ask the big questions about your worth and your future, you are immobilized by the fear of losing what little you have left.

And when it comes right down to it, in that place and moment, I was terrified that if anyone found out what was really going on, the house of cards would come crashing down and I would be left with the broken pieces. I repeated this story over and over to myself, reminding myself of all that was at stake if I didn't figure it out.

The Pain Prize

We sometimes cling to our pain like a prize, as if it is proof that we have a reason for why we keep on doing what we are doing. When we are trying to hide something, whether it be out of shame or as a matter of survival, smoke screens and shiny objects seem like logical strategies - at least they will seem like it at the time.

Perhaps one of the reasons we cling to our pain is rooted in pride. That was part of why I clung to pain for so long. I was going to fix it and make it all better than before, so why should I bother dealing with it? As long as it all went according to plan, the whole thing was going to pass by without notice.

I felt like I had everything at stake in this, and because I was all in, surely the universe would bend in my favour and give me what I wanted. And after it was all said and done, I would be the silent and gloating winner of the Pain Prize. I would proudly wear my secret badge, knowing that I had endured it all, had kept up a good front and had single handedly saved the world in the process.

But smoke screens eventually lift, and we inevitably have to deal with what is left behind. Hiding from the truth is a tactic that can serve us for a time, but eventually, truth will out.

And when it does, it will simultaneously be the worst and best thing that could have ever happened.

The Human Face of the "Go Around"

Looking back to those three painful years, I feel one emotion more than anything else: mental exhaustion. It was a daily juggling act to face the pain, stuff it back down, step out the door with a smile, and determine that I was going to change the world that day. There was so much to focus on other than the chaos of my private world that it was easy to feed my shiny-object addiction. I welcomed the opportunity to focus on something new and exciting because behind that front door there was only the same old pain, anger, destruction and darkness.

And who wants to be reminded of everything that needs to change or be fixed, right?

We live in world that is powered and fuelled by the pursuit of shiny objects. We have become so familiar with them that we have mistaken them for a comfort rather than building up the mental and emotional strength to identify them for what they really are. Shiny objects come in endless shapes and sizes. Sometimes they are blatantly shiny, but most times they are subtly seductive, whispering our name and telling us to just jump on board. They are tricky, and they are everywhere.

Social media is a shiny object that never seems to disappoint us in its ability to take our mind off of life. It can keep us so busy that we won't even realize that we have just lost five hours of life today that we will never get back. Social media exists in seemingly endless forms from online games to Facebook and Twitter, and my personal favourite, Instagram. No matter how many times we roll our eyes at people's photos of the "ultimate meal" that they just prepared, the 185 photos of their newborn, or their narcissistic self-portraits of them looking their sexiest, happiest and sparkliest, it's still so tempting to take just five more seconds!

We go to people's profiles and we see only what they want us to see - their happy and often carefully constructed glimpses of themselves and their world. We see their smiling families, their adoring partners, their always-cute kids and their quirky take on life. It's real and yet it hides the truth of who *we* really are. We check status updates on our smart phones while we are in the bathroom, on the train, or waiting in lineups at the bank. We hear about their newest adventures, their weekend plans and most of all, we are exposed to how much more exciting their lives are than our own. Everything about their world seems to be an endless adventure, and ours can seem like an endless amount of work and background noise that we don't want to deal with.

And when you are hurting, what looks ideal in their world only seems magnified against your own pain and disappointment. Still, the most confounding thing about it all is that the more we hurt, the longer we obsess over what is going on in other people's worlds. Like hidden paparazzi, we creep into other people's online lives instead of investing in our own. We count likes and comments as marks of approval and love, convincing ourselves that we are doing okay as long as everyone is entertained and fascinated with us.

But what's the story that we are really telling ourselves about all of this? That unless our lives are as exciting or dramatic as theirs we are missing out? What's resonating in your heart as you play the comparison game, chasing a shiny object like a puppy chases a reflection across the floor? Instead of being inspired by what we see, comparisons will only divert our attention to what's wrong with our lives, amplifying fears about who we are.

Confidence comes from knowing who we are, not from worrying about how we compare to someone else's glossy exterior.

Okay, time to get those naked confessions out there. I am sure you have never experienced this, so you can pretend this isn't you and just be shocked at what I am going to confess. Go ahead, feel safe and smug - I won't judge you.

I have created my own little term for something that followed me for many years. I like to call it the "shiny crush syndrome."

Life can get tedious at times. Routines can numb us into automating our lives, our relationships and our thought patterns. And then, something unexpected shows up (although it is rather predictable in the world of shiny objects).

You suddenly notice someone or something in a way that you never did before. Perhaps your attention was drawn because that person or idea inspired you or touched your life in a way that is endearing and remarkable. Your imagination has flared up, your views of the world are altered, and before you know you it, you are in full-on crush mode.

The shiny crush syndrome is something that is beyond the harmless attraction that will inevitably happen from time to time. It has the potential to overtake thought patterns and consume headspace. We can begin to wonder what life would be like "if." It can become too easy to become convinced that we are misunderstood, taken for granted, overlooked. Those convictions may even be real and valid, but those are separate issues from the issue of the shiny crush.

The shiny crush is about relationships we have with our own sense of significance. We can crush on people, on scenarios that we wish we were living in, or on a lifestyle that somehow seems to elude us. That's a dangerous and destructive game that never ends in wholeness; in the end, it only prolongs the brokenness. (Trust me on this one.) Escapism can be nice for a while, but eventually, we all need to come back to the real world and face what's happening in us and the lives we are privileged to live.

You deserve better. First decide to deal with what's in front of you rather than escaping into your imagination of what might happen "if."

My shiny crush syndrome haunted me for many years. I felt a mixture of shame and escapism through it all, because it didn't feel like it was congruent with who I was and the values I stood for. I wanted so much to be perfect and to convince myself that I was, that I didn't even have the guts to be honest with myself about where I was at. I have had many crushes over the years for many different reasons. I have crushed on people, on lifestyles that I thought I needed, and on scenarios I concocted in my imagination.

Crushes are cute - for a while. But eventually, there comes a time when we need to have the courage to be honest with ourselves and face life for what it is.

And life is good in its own unique way for each of us.

How Can I Afford Not To?

I have a joke with some girlfriends about when you see something on sale. The sale is way too good to pass up, so you justify it by saying, "How can I afford not to?"

Too bad my credit card company didn't share the same opinion!

For someone who has committed a big part of her life to fighting exploitation and injustice, I have my own secret battleground where I often fail to be stronger than my opponent. The mall.

Sometimes, as I glide through those double glass doors, I hear angels sing as they welcome me home, promising that I will feel better, look amazing and that my love-o-meter will be filled back up with retail therapy.

There have been a few critical points in my life where I have dealt with my pain and anger with a hellish vengeance as I shopped my heart out, throwing caution to the wind in a crazed attempt just to feel better. The shiny letters of my favourite retailers reached out to me, the accessories store sent vibrations of sparkly goodness my way, and even my favourite gadget store promised me that if I just stopped in and dropped $100, my life would be a lot richer for the experience.

They were right. I did feel a lot better. The high lasted while I walked around the mall, was pretty strong when I got in my car although it started to wane slightly as I drove home. And as I unpacked it all and laid it out on the bed, finally willing myself to face the total I had just spent, it didn't feel quite so shiny anymore.

Actually, it felt like I had to remind myself that I am an adult and I now needed to face my choices and figure out how I was going to pay for all of this. The "stuff" wasn't free, it came with a price tag. And even though I am a responsible consumer in terms of global choices, I still wrestle with doing all things in moderation.

I bet you thought I was going to pontificate on the evils of consumerism here, didn't you? Nope. Not going to happen. I have no right to rail away on the evils of "stuff" and materialism. There are so many great ideas, so many beautiful fashions that are a product of incredible insight and creativity, and so many ways to help the world be a better place that I can't go hard on it. I love it all.

But the difference for me is that I still love people more. Namely myself. And you.

We deserve more than shopping. We deserve peace of mind.

Retail therapy is actually quite intoxicating at times, within reason. And treating yourself is something that I wish everyone could do to be kind to themselves. But it still doesn't define me. It doesn't determine my value or worth because it's still just stuff in the end.

I think the danger lies in the process, because we never really find out what we like. Asking ourselves what we truly need or like seems to take too much time, and it's much easier and safer to just buy what everyone (namely retailers and pop culture) tells me I need rather than contemplating what I truly want or what I will be content with.

Do I think you should shop? Sure, go ahead. I do.

But for me, something has changed around why and how I do it. Shopping is enjoyable, but I don't let it be an escape anymore. I also don't pretend that my decisions don't matter. I choose to shop as ethically as I can, remembering that I am connected to other people's stories around the world.

I also choose to make choices that I can live with. Treating myself once in a while is different than searching for significance where it will never be found.

Does that once-in-a-while treat feel good? Yep, it sure does. Every. Single. Time.

When Being Busy Looks So Shiny...

Life has so many ebbs and flows, doesn't it? Sometimes you feel like you are so alive, so present and so in tune with where everything is going in your life. And then, other times, you feel as if you are lost, floating and trying to find your way back to where you feel you belong again. Sometimes when we are floating and feeling aimless we try to find things to occupy our time, to keep our mind off of things, to make us feel somehow useful. The flurry of busyness gives us the sense that we have somewhere to be, something to do, someone who is waiting on us, and all of that adds up to the veneer of feeling important. And everybody likes to feel important.

Busyness can be very exhilarating for me, and I sometimes do find clarity in the midst of it all as I have to make quick and sharp decisions and then move on. But being busy can also be an excuse not to deal with the chatter in my head and to hide behind what I tell myself I should be doing.

The crazy paradox of being busy is that it can actually be the biggest form of procrastination. Like a rush of adrenaline to our system, being busy can trick us into thinking that we are productive, that we are going places, and that we are important.

At times, the busyness we construct can help us avoid dealing with what the real issue at hand is. Busy families can avoid dealing with each other, busy couples can avoid having an honest and open conversation, and busy people can avoid the questions that quietness and solitude inevitably bring up.

If we stay busy, it's easier to avoid nagging doubts about the stories that we aren't ready to deal with. So instead of dealing with the nagging doubts, we construct stories around our busyness.

The fear of being honest with ourselves is far greater than the next adventure we are dreaming up! Being whole is never as exciting as partying and nothing ever makes us feel as needed as when we are working hard. Busy just feels so significant, so validating, so shiny.

Life gets busy — for all of us. Commitments, careers, relationships and interests all take time, effort and focus. We need them, we deserve them, we can find incredible fulfillment in them.

But we are intrinsically valuable beyond what we *do*. Beyond the question of "What do you do?", we can seek out the answers to the questions about who we *are*.

What Are We So Scared Of?

What could possibly be so bad about being honest with ourselves and allowing ourselves the chance to slow down, to listen for what we really need and to give ourselves the space and freedom to embrace that need? Well, I guess that depends on the story that you have told yourself around it all.

I am all about planning the next new adventure. I love planning epic vacations, weekend outings and spontaneous moments. After all, these experiences can be what keeps life fun and fresh. But when that next new adventure is because we don't want to stick around and clean up an old mess, then perhaps there is something more to consider. Jumping from one thing to the next is not going to help you grow or flourish.

In fact, it might only make you motion sick — and that's about as fulfilling as puking in the garbage bin outside the roller coaster line. You are worth the growth and depth of truth that can come from being willing to ask the bigger questions in life.

Being alone with your thoughts can be scary (I have truly been there) and it's sometimes easier to just keep on the run, maxing out your social life and staying occupied. But shiny objects eventually tarnish. They are best enjoyed with a healthy diet of honesty and integrity.

What story are you going to tell yourself about your shiny objects? Are you going to insist that they are harmless or are you going to put your foot down and make your story about the You that faced your fears and the unknown, and decided that you were worth the investment of seeing it through?

Try it. Life is way better on this side of it all.

P.S. This chapter took the longest for me to write. I actually found way too many exciting things to do for two weeks until I could bring myself back here to finish it.

Sigh...Shiny objects, I still heart thee.

Chapter 4:

My Sears-Catalogue-Lady Stint: Stories of Pain

I grew up on a farm. That farm came with wide, open fields, tractors and other farm machinery, a dog, innumerable cats, a pony, tonnes of cows, the odd skunk, a wandering bull, coyotes, and even a one-time celebrity appearance by a black bear.

Most people find my beginnings rather amusing if they know much about me. Mostly because I am just not the "let's take this tractor and take on the world" kind of girl. I am much more comfortable in stilettos than cowboy boots, and I would choose an urban jungle over a wide open space any day.

I didn't just grow up on a farm - I grew up on a farm in central Saskatchewan, where many farms are sometimes a kilometer or more away from their closest neighbor. Some days it seemed so quiet that you could hear the dandelion fluff floating into the sky.

Our house had a basement that stayed nice and cool in the summer when the heat was enough to make you cry on the main floor. We had an above-ground swimming pool, a massive garden, a shed for our car, a large shop where my Dad tinkered on projects, created dune buggies and go karts, and welded everything for himself and all the neighbors. There was a pop-up tent trailer that made its obligatory camping trips every summer, and there were massive grain bins on platforms that alternated between being full and waiting for the next harvest. The sky was wide and expansive in that place, and the northern lights danced in the deep cold nights of winter. Across the road, on a pond, I learned to water ski, all the while living in the fear of falling into the water and being consumed by the leeches that lurked just below the surface. We would skate on that same pond in the wintertime, sometimes having entire hockey teams full of cousins and neighbors out there.

Whenever I complained about being stuck on that farm, pining away for another existence somewhere far away, my parents would remind me of the many bonuses of my little world on that farm. They were right, of course. There weren't a lot of traffic jams, drive-by shootings (or shoutings for that matter), and there weren't a lot of worries about late-night noise - or any noise at all. There were, however, beautiful night skies, amazing sunsets, my bike, my little brother and my dog.

But here was the problem: I am an extrovert. And because of this unchangeable biological bent, I crave people and interaction. I can do no more to change that than the ocean can stop moving or the world can stop waging wars. It just is. I come alive with conversation, I dream of parties and laughter, and most of all, I crave human contact. I can't ever have too much of it.

In fact, when you are an extrovert, you are sustained, sharpened and refreshed by being around people. You thrive on conversation, connection and action. It's what you love more than anything else and it's hard to imagine living inside of a body that doesn't want to be around people and have meaningful conversations.

Those of us who are what I like to call "extreme" extroverts can also tend to be gifted/cursed with incredibly active imaginations. We love to dream up stories and we thrive on keeping people entertained and engaged. I think it comes partly from our need for an audience, and partly because we see life as an adventure, in full color. We love connections, but we are also okay with chit chat and happy and enlightening conversation. We love to make the rest of you feel that life is worth it and that we can show you how! Parties make our hearts sing, good conversation and wine fill up our love-o-meter, and we see each new person as someone to win over.

So Imagine the Dilemma...Of living on a farm in Saskatchewan!

I felt that I had no choice but to activate my hyperactive imagination in whatever extreme ways I could. When you're a kid that thrives on social outlets and you only ever dreamed of living in the city, you imagine yourself in that faraway place that you watched on *Sesame Street* and in every Disney movie that you voraciously consumed. You immerse yourself so deeply in those fantasies that the basement play area becomes a busy street, the garden plants become students you are instructing and inspiring to choose who they are going to be when they grow up, and the dog becomes that pretty, chatty friend you wish was there to play with every day.

But somehow, at the end of every day you have to face a reality: life has played a trick on you and you are still living on a farm where houses are a mile apart and the peer-interaction on most days is near zero.

I felt I had no choice in the matter, and it was an issue of survival in a cruel, quiet and pastoral world, so I did what I had to do: I invented an imaginary and alternate world of my own.

In that world I was the most glamourous person I could think of at the ripe age of five: I was the Sears Catalogue Lady. I would travel from one exotic locale to another, consulting and coaching my clients on fashion and helping them to make choices they would be happy with. I had a very impressive client list, filled with high-profile individuals and organizations. My clientele included the flower barrel, the dog and the cat, the power pole in the middle of the yard, and the fairies that lived behind the lilac bushes in our yard. They were all quite demanding at times, especially during the short flash-sale-catalogue seasons. But I was dedicated to bringing them the best service possible, and I did it with flair and style.

My adventures were limited by geographical constraints and I was allowed to ride my bike only on our property. To accommodate the customer demand, I would travel across acres of open fields and find a place to settle in with my clients and the catalogue. Together we would talk of our plans and I would consult with them on how to solve their problems. "We" created outfits and home decor that they could feel comfortable in and identified solutions that would help them in the days ahead. It was my first crack at coaching and consulting and I think that it was honestly the best job I ever had. I had interesting and engaged clients, I could take as long as I wanted for my breaks and everyone I worked with thought I was brilliant!

But at the end of the day, my little heart still craved interaction and face-to-face playtime with real people and real friends my own age. I wanted it so badly it would sometimes bring tears to my eyes.

For the extrovert, it's more than a focused discipline to have to spend any extended periods of time by yourself. It can be truly painful. You are sustained through connections, and those connections are how you process life, find your anchor points, sustain healthy views and keep your perspective. You don't just like to be with people, you are convinced your very survival depends on it. And in certain respects, it does.

Ask any extrovert what their personal hell is and they will undoubtedly tell you that it involves feeling left out, being forced to spend long hours alone (extremely challenging when you are a writer, by the way!), and losing connection with people that they care about. From the extrovert's point of view, these are very real pains and fears, and at times they can undermine our actions as we scramble to plan our world around not being alone. In our world, being alone is like putting a magnifying glass on emotional pain, as it withers under the sun, eventually catching fire and consuming itself.

Emotional pain comes in many forms. Sometimes it's subtle, and we function around it and through it without ever fully recognizing that it's there. Sometimes it's from a traumatic event and there is no denying its powerful effect on us. At times it just builds, moment upon moment, experience upon experience, until one day we wake up and have no idea how it showed up in our lives and how it seemed to consume our thoughts and actions. And whether we are introverts or extroverts, rich or poor, young or old, there is something about pain that we all share in common: we want to do anything we can to avoid it. Anything.

Emotional pain is a peculiarly unique state to deal with. In all forms, it seems to thrive on isolating its victims and giving them the illusion that they are alone through it all. Backed into a corner, we seem to find nothing else to focus on other than the obvious, most glaring thing we feel. However we arrived at this point of pain doesn't matter, because as long as it exists it will search out ways to convince us we are alone. If pain were a real being, it would thrive on this strategic move, time and time again.

When you feel like no one understands, pain wins.

When you refuse to reach out for help, pain wins.

When you refuse to forgive because there is no way you could ever possibly justify what that person did to you, pain wins.

Pain wins whenever we give up trying to understand the bigger picture, whenever we try to create a go-around and pretend everything is okay, and even when we allow it to cloud our judgments of those in our lives who don't understand what the big deal is and who encourage us to let something go or get over it.

Yanking Back the Curtains on Pain

Pain of any kind is just a feeling — nothing more. Although feelings are real, they are not necessarily the truth that we claim to seek. Feelings are only able to hold the power and truth that we assign them. They are actually dependent on following our lead, not the other way round.

When we allow it the freedom it's seeking, emotional pain will take on attributes that do not rightfully belong to something that is merely a feeling. Pain gains its power through this freedom to exist, and every time it returns to visit us, it can seem much stronger and more real than anything else.

As a feeling, pain can come through every possible means and experience. It happens differently each time, but it feels the same at the core. Pain loves to make us feel cut off, disconnected, judged, even misunderstood. Our feelings and reality may not be equivalent, yet somehow, in our moments of deepest pain, knowing all of these things can still make it hard to pull ourselves back to reality.

Because facing reality means facing the truth.

And that could actually mean not using pain as an excuse or diversion.

At the darkest times of my marriage, when things were so painful and I felt so lost, I would put my daughter, Widlene, to bed, go into the bathroom and curl up and cry on the cool, tiled floor. Many nights I cried myself into exhaustion, consumed with feeling hopeless, judged, and misunderstood. I felt so utterly alone in my dark world of pain. I thought that the pain itself was the reason that I felt this way, and I had become convinced that the pain was bigger and stronger than me. I was being crushed beneath my own pain and it was asphyxiating me.

The black hole seemed to grow more and more vast. I began allowing it to consume me. The questions taunted me all day long. I would question why God was angry at me, and then I would accuse Him of being unfair. I waffled between accusations and shameless begging. What had I done to bring all of this on? Had I not done enough good things to bring about a different result? Was I not aware of some rulebook that existed that I had violated?

My pain was very real and very consuming, but it wasn't just about the situation I was in at the time. My pain was resonating with something deeper inside of me, something that had me convinced that life was always unfair to me, that I was always going to have to fight for whatever I had.

It was a narrative I had constructed and I had to start to face the fact that I was the only one who could re-write it.

If we refuse to face our pain at its source, we unknowingly widen the gap between what we feel and what may be the reality. We might even be persuaded to let the barrier grow between us and other people that could help us. How could "they" possibly understand what we are going through? Who are they to tell us to just get over it, to move on, to be strong, to get some perspective? They have never been in our shoes or faced our difficulties and therefore, our assumptions were right all along: we are alone.

And so we reason with ourselves that no one understands. Negotiating for further pain in this circular chase, we reach an inevitable mathematical conclusion. As the gap grows between us and the others in our life, isolating us further, hope can dwindle. At least that's what it seemed like to me.

But I found out that pain only *seems* impenetrable. Every emotion has a weakness, something that can deflate it. I found the chink in pain's armour and that discovery meant the difference between despondency and the hope of rescue.

It's way too big a secret to keep to myself anymore.

Stopping the Blame Game

When we were kids, we blamed everybody else for everything.

"Who broke this?"

"It wasn't me; it was him!"

"Why did you just hurt your little brother?"

"It was his fault! He looked at me funny!"

The list goes on.

Blame is addictive.

I remember it being a sunny, quiet day (like most summer days on a Saskatchewan farm). We were in our pickup truck and my dad jumped out to go get something.

The only two left in the truck were Andrew and me. I was five, he was one. I was jealous, and he rained on my parade of having the attention and being able to do whatever I wanted. In that moment, I remember thinking, "You know what, Andrew? I don't really like you very much right now."

So I made a plan to prove my point. I was going to take matters into my own hands.

I pretended to see something out the window and said, "Hey, Andrew! What's this over here?"

And as he slid over to the window, I sneakily leaned over behind him and gave him a boost out the window. As he dangled from the window and tumbled down onto the ground (thankfully unhurt, only ticked off!) our dad came back out.

"What happened?" he asked, clearly scared.

"I don't know. He just jumped!"

It was always Andrew's fault, never mine. It was just easier to blame him for my actions than to reason through that my intentions might not be the best plan. The propensity to assign blame is an impossible trait to try to discipline out of a child and although it can make for funny or cute stories of childhood, it's not so cute when you grow up. Passing the buck gets kind of pathetic after a while. Yet we still do it!

We are so accustomed to finger-pointing and scapegoating that we are desensitized to taking responsibility for who we are. Facing our own actions and being humble enough to own them never comes naturally or gracefully. It's somehow just so much easier to make excuses to the world, to each other and, worst of all, to ourselves.

We are a culture of avid finger-pointers, characterized by pathetic and flimsy attempts to pass the buck and divert attention away from responsibility for our actions.

"If she didn't want to be assaulted and abused, she should have dressed/acted/behaved differently."

"I am this way because of my parents."

"I am wounded by what he did to me; I deserve to be a little selfish for a while."

"I wouldn't have talked so harshly to them and treated them that way if they didn't deserve it."

"I would make better consumer choices if the alternatives were cheaper and easier to access."

So much of our world can seem as if it's designed to keep us on the hamster wheel of blame and resistance to accountability. Instead of honouring who we could be by standing up and saying that we were wrong, that we are sorry or that we want to make things right, we are tempted to give in to something that only continues to rob us of who we are.

We are tempted to default to blame habitually because it provides us with a quick way to deal with our pain. It won't end without our decisive action to stop the cycle.

Perhaps we don't vocalize that blame all the time, but unless we make a conscious step towards letting it go, we will still live our lives and make our decisions in light of it. Blame can stay harboured in our hearts, as a card we feel justified in pulling out when we are in a bind or face consequences for our actions. Blame is so easy, so available and so convenient, yet the irony of this truth is that the more we use it, the further we get away from freedom.

I have fallen into the seductive arms of using blame as my way out. Way too many times to count, to be honest. And for me, the difference has always been how I have felt in the core of who I am when I am confronted about something. When I shoulder the responsibility or blame for something that is legitimately mine to take on, I feel different than when I try to create a smoke screen by passing the buck. Taking accountability for our actions definitely causes momentary discomfort, but it also creates the space to be free from long-term pain.

Because freedom comes in responsibility. When there is nothing left to hide, there is nothing for pain to hold on to anymore.

But Sometimes Life Still Isn't Fair

Even though we might try as hard as we can to be fair to ourselves and others, much of what we go through in life isn't fair. I wish it was. I wish that I could wave a magic wand and make everything fair in life. But I am no fairy godmother!

It's not fair that marriages and families fall apart. It's not fair that illness is no respecter of persons. It's not fair that the world is full of bigots and racists, bent on treating others with cruelty, judgment and stereotypes. It's also not fair that children are exploited, women are abused, and honest, hard-working people get taken advantage of it. It's not fair that we often forfeit precious time and energy by being consumed with trying to blame anything and everything for our pain instead of facing it and moving on. None of that is fair, and there is no excuse for it.

This is how Fair can Look:

Fair can look like living your life with complete wholeheartedness and embracing it in all its beautiful ugliness. Fair can look like being more than okay with who you are and it can be about living with the conviction that you are going to make it through whatever comes your way, one intentional step at a time.

Life is just as much about our decisions regarding who we are as it is about other people's actions or reactions. The decisions we actively make are ultimately what makes us grow, learn and choose who we want to become.

You and I are worth so much more than being victimized by our pain and allowing it to determine our actions and reactions, or allowing it to cloud our judgment and understanding of who we are. Does it really matter anymore who started what? Can you even remember the details with absolute certainty about that offence, that hurt or that event that threw you off course?

The ignorance or false assumptions of others is not our problem and we won't be able to change them through anger, sermons or accusations. Change comes from within each of us, according to our willingness. So let's be fair to *ourselves* and focus on what matters. And what matters is what we are going to choose about who we are.

Then One Day, Clarity Came

To be honest, my pain consumed me for a while. Looking back, it felt as if my sole focus had become about being rescued from the pain, the disappointment, the betrayal and the anger. The vortex of hurt was powerful, to say the least. In my humanness, I wanted the relief to come in a dramatic way. I began to fantasize about being lifted out of it all, and of tasting sweet, sweet vindication. I wanted life to give me back everything that it had stolen from me.

But it didn't happen.

Shocker, I know!

In fact, I got the opposite.

Instead of being rescued, I got clarity.

You may have thought that was a misprint, but yes, I said clarity.

That clarity showed up one afternoon when I felt like I was being pulled under by my personal pain and frustrations. My world had been systematically falling apart and

I was simply putting one foot in front of the other because I didn't know what else to do. One day, while working in a community in Dominican Republic with Live Different, I met a 60-year-old Dominican woman. She impacted me in ways she will never know. One simple conversation with her gave me insight on how to start to change my own story around pain.

Her story was like so many grandmothers around the world, left with nothing but her grandchildren and the harsh reality of providing for them on her own. The complete truth is that she just called them her grandchildren, even though there was no familial connection. She chose to become someone they could find safety and security with. Ultimately, she chose love over loss, and her life humbled me in its simplicity and openness. Her "grandchildren" had all been orphaned by AIDS and other evils. Taking those children in, providing for them, loving them and doing it all with peace and acceptance gave her almost super-human qualities to me. She was Dominican yet she took in Haitian orphans. In a world and community where these two cultures rarely mixed, her life shone light on what love really was, and illuminated all around her with the gift of kindness. Her story and character challenged me and shook me to the core. Her kindness illuminated my path in some way I will never be able to explain.

As I talked to her, I saw that not only was she a strong and capable woman, she was also kind and able to embrace life for what it was. Had it been unfair to her? Sure. But her approach was basically, "So what?" Sitting around and bemoaning the fact that life was unfair wasn't going to change the situation in front of her. The situation at hand demanded resolute decision making, and the only person who could begin to change it was her.

Her actions spoke more to me than any words I had tried to find to express how I felt. They reached deep into my soul and begged to be reckoned with. I went back to my apartment that afternoon after I had met her and walked into the bathroom.

I stared at the face looking back at me and began to ask questions that I had been too afraid to ask before. Questions about why I had allowed my pain to give me tunnel vision. Why had I allowed myself to get so small in my thinking, when I knew I was made for so much more? When had I stopped giving myself permission to grow and learn, and instead begun to shrink and hold out on life?

Asking myself these difficult questions allowed me to come face to face with the truth: I wasn't who I thought I was, I was capable of so much more.

Over the days that followed, I couldn't get my encounter with that lady out of my mind. It began to haunt me and challenge me to see my own world differently. In turn, it began to push me to see myself differently.

I had been captivated with a sense of entitlement that hurt me more than helped me. I had allowed my pain to isolate me. To my shame, I had allowed my own pride to get in the way of reaching out. I felt that too many people were depending on me and too many consequences were resting on my shoulders. I had decided that I could handle it on my own, but all that I managed to do was fool myself. My pain had been enabled through my need for control and my thirst for justification.

That was a losing battle no matter how hard I tried to convince myself otherwise.

A few nights after meeting that lady, sitting alone in my bedroom, I decided it was time to change the story I was telling myself. I decided I needed to stop looking over my shoulder and pointing a finger. It was time to decide what kind of story I was now going to create from this point forward.

It was about the Questions

When we are in pain, we have endless questions. Why me? Why them? Why now? Why?

When something happens in our bodies, we ask why it had to happen right then.

When a circumstance sideswipes us, we ask, why weren't we in a different place, at a different time?

We ask for relief from anywhere we can get it.

Because we are good people— and bad things shouldn't happen to good people, right?

I felt this jab the sharpest. I was a freaking humanitarian, for crying out loud! What kind of cruel joke was this?

But those kinds of questions, although the natural response to pain, are not the right questions to ponder if we are looking for a way out of the pain. Those are questions that will only confuse us and corral us into a circular thought pattern with no break in the loop.

The truth is that the question I had never considered asking until that day when I met that woman (much to my own embarrassment) was "Why not me?"

How did I arrive at a place where I thought that I should get a free pass on pain and suffering? I had bought into a lie that took a long time to uncover inside of me. I had grown arrogant about my suffering and things had to change.

I had to change me first. I was one of millions of people around the world working through a situation I didn't ask for. I didn't bring it on, but it showed up, so now I had the opportunity to choose what to do with it.

I could make the decision that day to move consciously towards choosing the story of hope over the story of pain. It was time to embrace the reality that I am part of something bigger and better than where I momentarily found myself. It happened one small step at a time.

Clinging to pain was exhausting. Justifying my reactions to pain stole my peace and focus and I was ready to have it back. So I changed the story I told myself about where life had brought me. I wasn't alone, I was on a journey and there were people there that I could reach out to. I wasn't above getting help and getting objective perspective and I couldn't use the "being in the public eye" and "people are depending on me" excuses anymore. I was going to come to terms with this pain and I was going to decide who I was in the midst of it — and in spite of it.

"Faith is taking the first step, even when you don't see the whole staircase." ~ Martin Luther King Jr.

When your pain is the first thing you talk about, think about, or consider, you aren't just someone who is in the middle of a difficult life circumstance; you are someone who is reveling in all that is wrong with your life. And if you are wearing it like a badge of honour (even if it's just in front of the bathroom mirror) your pain is finding a pleasant little partner to settle in with: Pride.

(Yuck. I hate having to admit when I have been prideful. It hurts my pride!)

But I, too, had been prideful. I had shrunk my worldview down to the base level of my pain and adversity. And I was the only one who could do anything to change it.

So where could I start?

At first it took an incredible amount of effort to re-focus my attention. I found that the path of least resistance had been when I was clicking on the default mode of the old stories of my pain and injustice.

But I had to reclaim my energy and find what I really wanted to resonate with again.

Every time I was tempted to go there in my mind (every 5 minutes on some days!) I began to stop myself and remind myself that there was so much more of my life left to embrace, enjoy and be present to.

I decided to look at my life for what it was: a gift, an opportunity and a legacy.

And the best thing happened in front of my eyes.

I found peace and understanding in the story of Christal.

In the end, I found justice.

It had been hiding in plain sight all along.

In the innocence of childhood, there was a much more accessible path to resilience. It somehow seemed easier not to dwell on pain because we didn't yet have a world view shaped by it and we were easily distracted from disappointments by other more enticing activities.

I have often wished I could find my way back to the time in my childhood when I could effortlessly step into another reality I created and the simple pleasures it built for me. But until someone successfully bends the time continuum and we can go back, the endless blessing of life is that we get to choose how we will interpret our circumstances, our experiences and our relationships as we move forward. We determine their significance and the weight they hold for our future.

And the future can look very, very good.

Chapter 5

Fergie and the Easter Eggs: Stories of Failure

I love Easter. Easter equals a fresh start in my world, and fresh starts are always exciting for me.

There is something so exhilarating about Easter when you grow up in the northern half of the northern hemisphere. The very word, *Easter*, evokes thoughts of spring and freshness, fluffy, baby chicks, Cadbury Easter Cream Eggs, new dresses and shoes, Easter egg hunts, and shiny little shoots of green that begin to poke through the scenery all around you.

For those of us who grew up celebrating Easter, there were always the unknowns surrounding the celebration, questions that begged to be answered. Where does the Easter bunny get his chocolate? How did he and Jesus fit into the mix? How does "he" lay eggs? Does he have opposable thumbs so that he can carry the baskets around?

These were the thoughts I was focused on when I decided our Hero Holiday team was going to celebrate Easter in northern Thailand with 125 kids and staff in one of the best places on earth: a children's home for kids rescued from slavery and sexual exploitation. It's a place of healing, a place of hope and a place of new beginnings. It's one of the places in the world that truly owns a little piece of my heart. It's a place of raw beauty - the kind of beauty that leaves you breathless because of how it has come into being. And one of my favourite things to do when I am there is to plan activities that celebrate the beauty in their lives and their stories of freedom and redemption.

So when I planned for this particular little excursion, I had all of those intentions in mind.

As we plotted out the day, we tried to plan it through the eyes of those children and envision how they would feel about an Easter egg hunt. What would tantalize their senses and fill them with laughter and wonder? What would give them the best feeling of lightness, joy, and belonging? How could we make it a challenge but not impossible for them?

Okay, to be truthful, there were a few things un-Easter about the set-up. First of all, most of these kids weren't even Christian. Or Jewish, for that matter. They were actually mostly Buddhists and tribal religions from northern hill tribes in Thailand and Myanmar. But they were kids, and what kid doesn't want an adventure? They don't care what the religious attachment is to a celebration, they just care that we are celebrating something — anything — and that the celebration involves candy and games.

That's why, that morning, I was confident of what the day ahead held for all of us. This was going to be a fantastic day, and our team was about to experience something so amazing and full of joy that the feeling for all of us who participated would last long after the day was over.

I was right, it was memorable, but what I didn't know was that there would be some unexpected memories attached to it as well. Memories that, to this day, still make all of us laugh with incredulity at the whole experience.

Earlier that morning, we bought out the local 7-11 with all the non-meltable candy they had in stock. Back at our hotel property, we made a plan with the team. Our hotel sat next to a small, quiet lake, on a rambling property that gently sloped down toward the water. The property was full of trees, massive areas of green grass and low-lying bushes. It was a perfect and picturesque location for an Easter egg hunt. This was going to be amazing!

We were probably one of the biggest groups the hotel had hosted in a long time. For starters, the hotel was kind of off the grid, at the end of a long, quiet road outside a small, sleepy town. They were clearly appreciative of our business and they were determined to do their best to anticipate our needs and requests. I truly appreciated their attentiveness and effort, despite the regular tendency for things to get lost in translation and cultural interpretation.

In particular, I remember initiating a conversation with the manager earlier in the week about breakfast, asking if we could have hot cereal, such as oatmeal, as an option for our team to choose from. When we talked, he nodded enthusiastically and smiled, giving me the impression that everything was understood.

But when we came down at 6:30 the next morning and breakfast was soup broth with fish heads floating in it, I realized that we had somehow not managed to connect on the issue.

I should have remembered that as we planned the Easter egg hunt together.

When our little army of guests finally arrived late in the afternoon, already 90 minutes late, I was worried we would run out of daylight for their hunt. We hustled them all to a cleared-out area at the top of the hill and asked them all to sit down for a moment, as we handed out small plastic bags.

I began my instructions, working with the translator and using crazy hand gestures to get the point across.

"Ok everyone, guess what?" I asked, trying to build the anticipation.

"Back home in Canada right now, children are still sleeping, dreaming about what you are about to do!"

I could see curious eyes light up, and as their little hands started to fidget with the bags, they leaned forward to hear what we were going to do.

"Today is Easter Sunday. Easter is about celebrating the goodness of life, the love of God for us and about how all things can be made new. In Canada, lots of kids like to celebrate Easter with a special party. It's called an Easter Egg Hunt! And because you guys are some of the greatest kids in the world, we thought it would be so cool if you could be the first kids in the world this year to go on an Easter Egg Hunt, searching for the best and the most candy you can find all over this property!"

Now there was a visible vibration in the air, as understanding swept across the crowd. Even the workers began to giggle with the anticipation and excitement of our theatrics. I told them I would count to ten and then the music would start. They would have 15 minutes to race around and collect as much candy as possible, wherever they could find it.

I looked over at the hotel staff member who gave me the thumbs up from beside the massive, powered speaker that he had plugged a tiny MP3 player in to. He was waiting for my signal to start playing our mood music. Earlier I had told him to play something that children would enjoy and relate to, specifically asking for something that was celebratory, danceable and light hearted.

However, thinking we were on the same page about appropriate music for kids, Easter Egg Hunts and family events, I didn't specify what kind of dancing I had in mind. That was my mistake.

The countdown began, the chanting of numbers grew louder, and as we reached "go," the kids all screamed and jumped up, scrambling around to find sugary treasures as they laughed, rolled and wrestled on the lawn all around us. It was beautiful. As tears trailed down my cheeks, I thought my heart would burst with the sensation of such pure joy and innocent abandon.

I gave the thumbs up to my "DJ" and got ready for a Disney-esque moment of rapturous music to make the moment complete. Instead, what we got was a shock, as we heard Fergie and Will-I-Am start to banter through the blasting speakers about all "that junk" in somebody's "trunk" and getting "love-drunk" off of something they referred to as "humps"!

I stood frozen and in shock that we now had 125 children running around and collecting Easter eggs to the music of "My Humps." I was speechless as I turned around and looked at the DJ. He just smiled and waved, giving me his usual thumbs-up. From his perspective, we were on the same page of understanding, and he was loving the moment, assuming I was enjoying it just as much.

Ever since that day, I have always wondered if an artist envisions their music at a certain type of event. If so, I bet the Black Eyed Peas couldn't have ever foreseen that one. If it had been a tweet, the music choice would have been #epicfail.

But the kids and the staff didn't even notice. Most of them didn't even understand English, and the musical choice was of no consequence to them. They were just glad to show up and live in the moment. They were safe, they were alive and they were loved. Who cared whether everything went according to plan and that to my extreme disappointment, embarrassment and frustration it didn't go as I had envisioned it? It was a raging success from the perspective of the people who mattered: the little hands frantically scrambling for candy treats across that hillside that afternoon in northern Thailand.

I was embarrassed about how the music got bungled up, and in particular about playing that exact choice of music around kids who had been rescued out of exploitation. I was wasting precious moments beating myself up about not clarifying things better when I met with my DJ, and I lost out on all the amazing gifts of being present to the experience in front of me. The failure screamed louder than the success of what was happening right in front of me. I unknowingly perpetuated something in me that I will continue to wrestle with all of my days: the continual push and pull of living between my expectations around what I want to happen, and celebrating it as it happens. My obsession with failure can sometimes hold me captive, even blinding me to my own success.

Failure is More About Perception Than we Realize

The perception of failure is very rarely about the event itself. It's way more about the stories we build around those moments and how we allow them to become what we tell ourselves.

This moment was definitely about the story I told myself. While I stood there, looking out across the picturesque hotel property on that lake, I cringed and felt ashamed of the music that pumped in the background behind me, encouraging the world to focus on something that wasn't quite as innocent as Easter eggs, in a tiny microcosm of the world that needed to regain innocence by any means possible.

I had failed to communicate what we wanted, but as I looked around at our team, they were all either too busy wrestling and squealing with the kids as they hunted for sugary treasures, or crying tears of laughter at the hilarity of our musical theme. The story they were all telling themselves was of joy, laughter and pure love.

That was a much better story and I decided I wanted to remember that story instead.

I have spent a lot of my life rating and ranking everything by comparisons. Most of those comparisons revolved around how I felt I measured up to the world around me.

When we started what has now become known as Live Different, we didn't have a clue about how to do anything. Our passion, drive and boundless optimism overrode everything else, including wisdom. In the end, that passion and drive would be what I clung to during the hardest times, when we were in survival mode. There was so much that was done the hard way, and so much that I wished we would have done differently.

Live Different came to represent everything that defined me, everything that I was capable of bringing to the world. It was almost impossible to separate myself from it, as I was wrapped up in it from every possible angle. I had sacrificed everything I had to give it enough push to exist for just a little bit longer. Day by day, we survived on hope, prayer, and the sheer determination to exist another 24 hours. There was a resolute, unwavering passion to make it succeed, to accomplish great things, and to change the world. We were convinced that the world needed us to survive, that lives would be changed if we hung on, and that we needed to persevere.

I will always believe that to be true. Thousands of lives that have been impacted by our programs and people are proof of that. But Live Different was never intended to be about me or my dreams, it was about creating a space for people to discover what they were capable of accomplishing.

For a long time I was incapable of understanding the difference or seeing the real meaning of Live Different for what it truly was. I had put everything on the line to make this exist, I had sacrificed my own life on the altar of hope, and I had chosen the hard way in everything, believing it was the only way. My life and my own significance had become inextricably entangled with the mission of the organization I had helped to create and sustain.

But all that time there was something lurking just beyond where I was at, waiting for me to stop for a moment.

It was the feeling of failure, and at times it drove me to despair at the thought of what it could do to me. Sometimes I shed so many tears over potential failure that it seemed they would never stop.

If we allow it the freedom, failure will hang onto us, clinging to our every thought, every word, every step, reminding us of what we did wrong. But failure is actually always on the lookout for a way to evolve and to grow. Like every other emotion we encounter, failure's importance and strength will evolve in the direction we nurture it. But make no mistake, it will evolve.

Because of failure's nature, it cannot remain static; like flowing water, it needs to pour into something, somewhere. And that is where we can often miss the opportunity to watch it evolve into something that serves us rather than enslaves us.

"Failure is an event, not a person." - Zig Ziglar

Our human nature often wants us to see failure not as something we did wrong, but as something that is inherently wrong with us. Our need to connect and identify can often lead us to identify with the failed event, relationship or attempt, rather than the opportunity for growth, insight and freedom that can come from that failure.

I have failed. Miserably, actually. But it wasn't that failure that defined me, it was my act of taking that failure on as my own. In fact, by choosing to take that failure personally, I let that failure define me. My fear of admitting, let alone embracing, my failures made me averse to confronting what wasn't working in my life and relationships. When I panicked about Live Different potentially not succeeding, I focused on getting people to love me and believe in me, thus diverting my attention from the unknown of facing the failure.

(I know, brilliant long-term strategy, right?) Ha!

Looking back, it seems almost ridiculously simple how much easier and more peaceful I could have made my life. The simple choice to reach out for help, to slow down and allow myself the opportunity to really and truly see what it was that I needed to grow could have changed a lot of things. But I was incapable of seeing the forest for the trees. My ego was so wrapped up in my work and in identifying myself with what I did, that I couldn't separate myself from it. If Live Different failed, I was convinced that its failure would be my own, and in some ways, I think I wrote out the plot line before it ever happened.

So foolish and short sighted. So human. Sigh.

What if, like everything else in our lives and stories, failure is defined in how we identify it? What if we are the ones who get to decide how to assign meaning to what happens, by what we do, and by taking responsibility in a healthy way? How would that change and shape the stories we create around ourselves?

I think the story would be very different and the way it would be retold over and over again could actually serve to help us learn, to empower us and to set us free from hang-ups that are not ours to get hung up on.

Failure is the only way to redemption, and redemption might be one of the most painstakingly beautiful experiences of our earthly existence. If failure truly is found in how we identify it, then the stories surrounding our lives need to line up with that truth. Giving ourselves the grace to remember that failure is an event and not a life sentence changes our perspective and allows us to stay hopeful that we don't have to find our identity in it.

Maybe a failed relationship is not about everything that is wrong with that other person, but what we can learn about who we can become and bring to all the other relationships in our lives.

Maybe a failed business venture isn't about a money failure, but a chance to defeat your fears about stepping out and being willing to try something, even if it doesn't turn out how you want it to.

Maybe it is about making it a catalyst for a different future.

A different you.

A different story.

The Un-Sexy Tango with Failure

The story of the adoption journey with my daughter, Widlene, may look like a tangled mess from the outside. In the beginning, it seemed like such a simple answer to a crisis that stranded an innocent child. A failed attempt to fast track a visa led to a colossal mess. An earthquake destroyed all possibilities of paperwork that was started and a country closed its doors because we didn't fit the prototype. Shortly after, as my marriage began to disintegrate, I became stranded between two countries in an effort to hold my job and child together in my life. I have wasted thousands of dollars that I did not have trying to find the right lawyers, connections, and inroads, all to end up in a place that the world would consider further away from where I started.

Well-meaning people have meted out judgment on everything from reminding me that God is in control and that the problem is that I probably got in the way (irrelevant if He is really in control, don't you think?), to telling me how selfish it is to not fight for my marriage because of all the instability it has caused.

And here is my personal favorite: Have you ever thought of just sending her back?

Honestly, people have said that. Clearly, loving someone is not enough in their eyes to make the sacrifice worth it. (Never mind the fact that they would never have said that to someone whose biological child was in the same situation.)

And all of those things could have piled up, end over end, to result in being crushed under feelings of failure. And they did, for a time.

But they don't anymore.

As I write this book, I still have no answers -- only more questions. I don't know how it will end or if it will turn out the way I wish. But we don't know how anything will end, do we? I may succeed at what I set out to do. But I might also fail. Either way, I now understand that there is more to the story than what my experience or emotions have led me to believe.

When I decided that failure was going to become about how I interpreted the situation and what I could learn and grow into, my line of sight changed. It became less about what I saw in the immediate view and more about the bigger picture.

My future potential is still a white canvas waiting for all the possibilities of what it can become.

And so is yours.

We Grow Into Ourselves...

Like shoots reaching for the sun, not yet able to see our full potential, we reach out and grow up. Along the way, we make some mistakes. Some little ones and some colossal ones. All the while we are growing into who we are becoming.

Growth is difficult, scary and most of all, inevitable. Life is process after process. Biologically, spiritually, intellectually, and emotionally, we are always going to grow into ourselves, and then soon find ourselves needing bigger sizes, bigger vessels, bigger dreams. Our capacity expands with our willingness to let it happen. Along the way we are making attempts at trying to figure it out, to find our way and to see how we fit into it all. Failure is not one of the mortal setbacks of that expansion -- it's a vital part of the framework of growth that we need in our life to shape us and bring out the full potential that each of us possess. Our failures can be the very thing that give us the insight and grace for ourselves and others to grow and learn.

When I was little, I remember getting clothes for Christmas or my birthday, and they were inevitably just a little bit too big for me. When I really liked the clothes, it was a little disappointing to know that they didn't yet fit exactly as I wanted them to. However, I remember hearing this reminder every time I complained about it to my Mom: "Don't worry, you'll grow into them soon."

And I did. Every single time. (Thankfully it's not that way now! I am done growing, thank you very much.)

I remember putting on the dresses and it would make my eyes sparkle, just knowing that they were mine. Even though they weren't quite the exact right fit for me just yet, I still wore them. I wasn't very much bothered by it, because in the end, I am a fashionista, and all that really mattered was that I was wearing what I wanted!

Every time I face a new challenge, a new direction, a new opportunity that I know I don't want to let pass me by, I think of those dresses. I think of being a kids size 6X and wearing that size 8 anyway — because I loved that dress, and I wanted to get the most out of it. And when you want something badly enough you will find a way to make it work.

What is the bird's eye view of your situation?

It's so easy to get caught up in the tangles and snarly emotions of our individual history. Pulling ourselves back and seeking perspective will change everything.

What can you do to get perspective on your own situations and challenges? What points of view do you need to consider to reframe a particular part of your story?

And, better yet, what can you learn from your failures and the power of re-framing them into assets in your life, your journey and your story?

To not take anyone or anything for granted? to trust your gut instinct more? to listen to the critics a whole lot less? that you can't control other people, you can only ultimately choose who you are?

When you fall flat on your face there is nowhere to go but up. And that isn't necessarily a bad thing.

Seriously, you can trust me on this.

I have a heckuva lot of first-hand experience!

The Failure to Launch

There have been times when I have doomed ideas or plans before they ever took on form or shape. It's one of the things about being Christal that has frustrated me over the years. Ideas have come to me that were waiting for me to take action on. They were really great, really solid ideas and it was so easy to become enamored with the ideas in and of themselves. I would dance with them in my mind for a while, playing them out and imagining them coming to pass, getting excited at all the possibilities they held. Oh, the anticipation!

And then, just when I was about to take what I would consider to be the first legitimate step toward pursuing them, it would happen.

The fear of failure.

I didn't even get out the door and I was already running back inside!

The fear of failure is the stuff of legends when it comes to psychological inquiries, but when it comes down to it, the fear of failure is about a story that we fabricate. When we allow ourselves to succumb to a fear of failure, we are imagining a future that hasn't happened yet and we are deciding on our own that it is going to disappoint. We do the most ridiculous thing imaginable: we make our present-day decisions on unknown factors in the future.

For the record, I also think that this is why so many people find fault with the weatherman and economists. We want guarantees that the weather and our money will do what we want them to and it is unnerving to think that life is full of variables. But rogue circumstances happen all the time. Who can predict where lightning will strike, when someone will take one second too long to make a left-hand turn at a stop light or when one too many butterflies will flap their wings and start a hurricane.

The only thing we can be certain of is the "certain fact" that life will bring changes.

Why do we fear failure? Why are so many of us prone to giving in to that fear, weighing out the level of commitment and work it will take and passing judgment on the idea before it even gets a chance to defend itself or prove its worth?

Perhaps we fear what we can't understand and put into our own context. Ultimately, I think we fear what we will find out about ourselves in the process.

Spanish Zero

I have worked and traveled back and forth to Dominican Republic for ten years, In fairness, the first five of those ten years were very limited in their scope and I was always working with English teams and translators wherever I was. However, I had put off learning Spanish for way too long. I spoke some Spanish, but I was unable to communicate clearly what I wanted or needed outside of simple child-like phrases. I made up all kinds of excuses, all of them lame, as to why I didn't properly learn Spanish: I didn't have time, I didn't have the right teacher, I was a poor language learner, blah blah blah.

The truth is, I told myself I wouldn't be able to do it. I told myself I would fail before I even tried. I would limp through conversations with a cute laugh and ridiculous hand gestures, lamely hoping that my charm would communicate everything for me. All because I was freaked out by the idea of failing at learning the language and that I would have another humiliating experience in a grocery store.

Good grief, that sounds ridiculous, doesn't it? I had decided I was a Spanish zero before I even gave myself the chance to test the theory!

The story had to change about what I told myself about my abilities to learn Spanish. It had to become about the possibilities rather than the limitations. It's amazing how taking one small step towards what intimidates us can alter our perspective.

I found a teacher and I started to tell myself that I was capable of learning. I started to imagine how my world would open up if I learned this language: all the connections and conversation, all the possibilities, like not being scared of being lost because I would actually be able to ask for directions.

And, to my amazement, I am learning much more than I ever gave myself credit for. From zero to practically hero in such a short time — well okay, maybe not quite "hero" but at least "growing learner!"

Should I be surprised that changing the story changed my perspective? Hardly.

What stories are resonating in you around your failures? How are those stories directing how you define yourself, your potential and your future?

If you have told yourself that you feared failure, maybe try asking yourself a different question: Is it that I fear failure or is that I don't know how to see myself as separate from that failure?

Failure is a momentary state — but you and I are here for the long haul. We deserve the freedom that comes from the adventure of stepping out. It might work, it might not. You won't know the answer until you try.

And even then, it's all about what you decide about who you are.

Yep, Zig, you were right. Failure *is* an event *not* a person.

And I, for one, am incredibly glad to resonate with that story.

Chapter 6

Monkey-Bar Trauma: Stories of Shame

The first eight years of my education were spent attending a country school.

Not the kind where I walked uphill both ways in the snow all year round. (However, my dad has always insisted that was the case when he was a kid.)

Nevertheless, it was in the country. Our school property was massive, complete with an outdoor ice rink, four ball diamonds, and a wide open field that was used for soccer, football, track and field and lacrosse. It also had a large playground with an enormous jungle gym, teeter-totters, tetherball and massive swing sets with swings that made you feel you could touch the sky when you were little.

There were no shortages of places to play, wonders to discover or kids to chase around in a game of tag. That was a good thing, because our wait time for the bus was sometimes half an hour after school. Living in the country meant your world was tied to the school bus schedule. And my wait for the bus was a long one.

I got on the bus at 7:40 in the morning and got home at 4:20 in the afternoon. When your world is elementary school, hide-and-seek and figure-skating lessons, that's a long day to be filled with many different activities. Not a lot sticks out in your mind at the end of the day, but there was one particular encounter that was very memorable.

I remember exactly how it happened. It was shortly after the final class ended for the day. The bus wouldn't be there for another 15 minutes and I was free to do the business of being a kid: conquering a new area of the jungle gym and letting off the last bit of my energy.

When I got there, Ben (*not his real name) was already there, hanging upside down and doing what boys do best. Showing off. Ben was always teasing me, and in fact, he probably teased most of the girls in our class. He seemed to not have a filter or know when enough was enough. Looking back, I realize that he was always in the resource room, getting extra help with his work because he never quite seemed to catch up to the rest of us. Because he was held back in first grade, he was a year older than everyone else in our class. He was the one at the disadvantage, but in grade four I didn't pay much attention to those details.

I definitely never paid much attention to him either, because he annoyed me, and I avoided him like the plague. However, that day he followed me around the playground, refusing to leave me alone. According to my measurements, he took his teasing too far.

As I was hanging upside down and congratulating myself on my new feat, Ben came up to me, getting close to my face.

"You know what, Christal?" he asked as I could feel all the blood draining to the tip of my head.

"What?" I replied.

"You have big craters in your forehead. You are an ugly crater-face."

And then he walked away, leaving me there to deal with this new revelation.

I came down from the monkey bars and ran into the bathroom to look at myself in the mirror. He was right, I did have massive craters in my forehead. Big, ugly scars, left over from my bout with chicken pox when I was two years old. I had never noticed them before, never felt self-conscious about them until I stood there and let his words sink in.

How could I have missed the obvious? I was so ugly, so imperfect, so scarred.

Careless words spoken on the playground altered my perception of who I was.

Careless words that made me feel ashamed of how I looked, ashamed of something I couldn't change, ashamed of something that made me feel imperfect.

Ben was never my friend. In fact, I don't even remember him having many friends in school because of his aggression and difficulty in connecting with other kids. But in my 10-year-old mind, none of that mattered. All that mattered was how I felt about something that he said, a barb that went in like an arrow and refused to let go. It was the shame of being convinced that there was something wrong with me, something that made me different, ugly and not worthy.

The monkey-bar incident so profoundly impacted me that, from the time I was 10 until I was well into high school, I always tried to wear my hair over my forehead, to hide my shame of being imperfect. Shame that was attached to something I couldn't even control or change. I was two years old when I got chicken pox. It wasn't my fault. But somehow, shame doesn't ever seem to know the difference, whether something was our fault or not. It just is.

Shame. Yuck.

Just the word alone holds incredible meaning for many of us. We can feel shame at how we look, shame at our physical limitations, shame about what happened in our family or inside of our home, shame at where we came from, and shame at our actions in the past. We can feel shame at the thoughts that float around in our heads, shame at being different, and shame at whatever cultural differences define us. We can often even succumb to feeling shame at bad things that happen to us, wondering if we somehow attracted it into our lives. It's even possible that some of us can feel a bizarre sense of shame at wanting more for ourselves and for our innate desire to seek out more fulfillment and depth in our lives.

Shame is a powerful frequency to tune in to.

In the context of choices and consequences, the fact that we feel shame, to a certain degree, manages to keep our actions and attitudes in check and allows us to be mindful of ourselves. However, shame is only healthy when it brings a resolve to take responsibility for something we have done that we need to acknowledge is wrong. When it plagues us to be ashamed about something that we had no control over, shame has crossed the line. Because shame never knows when enough is enough. Shame on you, shame.

Shame loves the dark.

Darkness is hard to define. In the physical, it means the absence of light and it opens up all other possibilities for evil — or at the very least, questionable intentions. Terrible things happen in the dark. Terrible things that we may not want to speak of or think about ever again. Scary things can manifest, as the darkness somehow creates a fertile breeding ground for fears and the unknown. We can imagine we hear and sense things in the dark that may or may not be real. Darkness pulls on our weaknesses, casting doubt on our ability to find our way and causing us to stumble around without clear direction.

At times, darkness is a world of unknown and unthinkable possibilities. Perhaps that's why it represents so many other fears and anxieties for some of us. Under the cloak of darkness, hidden from daylight and understanding, nothing is clearly seen and perceptions can be distorted.

Shame loves the dark.

Darkness is just so welcoming to shame. Perhaps it's because many of our associations with feelings of shame also revolve around feelings of confusion, betrayal, or intense, paralyzing fear of something that happened to us. Maybe it's all of those reasons and more. Maybe it's because darkness is also a place where we go in our minds to tuck things away that we don't want to deal with. Hiding something we have done or that has been done to us can haunt us, making us somehow feel that everyone can see that there is clearly something wrong, something unacceptable or something that is damaged within us. But we also fear coming clean; we fear that revealing our secret will mean a future that is filled with even more shame than we already carry.

Inevitably, when the darkness cloaks the shame long enough, we somehow cross a line from feeling that there is something wrong with us to being firmly convinced that there *is* definitely something wrong with us. Something that would cause others to judge and reject us if they knew about it. All because our shame has convinced us that *we* are what's wrong, and there is no longer a separation between us and the actions that happened.

Yep, if I was shame, I would want to make sure things stayed hidden in darkness, too. It's the perfect alibi and the perfect vantage point for control of the situation.

You Know It's Out There, Somewhere...

Have you ever noticed how your senses seem to pick up on things in the dark that never seemed noticeable in the daylight? The sounds of a house or building shifting and settling are so evident in the dark, at times seeming ominous and threatening. When we wander around a familiar place in the dark, cognizant of the lack of light that restricts our vision, it can seem hard to picture that familiar place as being welcoming and comfortable. It suddenly seems to be a place of suspicious noises and feelings. A place where you are scared of what you will find around the next corner, even though you have been around that corner thousands of times in the daylight.

And that same kind of darkness is where shame hides out in our minds and in the very stories that we tell ourselves about who we are.

Shame works to convince us that darkness is the best place for it to communicate:

> *"Don't let the world know, because you know how they will look at you differently."*
> *"There are so many people depending on you. What would they do if they knew the truth about you?"*
> *"You know he wouldn't have done that to you if you hadn't been so easy."*
> *"You secretly liked it."*
> *"You don't belong here. Remember where you came from?"*
> *"You will never be as good or smart or accepted as they are."*
> *"You really don't fit the image that everyone else in this group is in to."*
> *"Who do you think you are?"*

The list could go on and on, an endless tirade of thoughts that we feel are better left in the dark and tucked away. We tell ourselves we aren't affected by it and we go to great lengths to try to convince our greatest doubter: Us.

Like a larger-than life film, we play our movie or story over and over in our head, living it out in front of the world, according to what we want them to see and know. And yet, all the while, we have our own outtake reel continuing to play and compare us to everyone else. But the thing is, we are seeing their edited version too. In the end, none of us are much different at all. We are all just trying to find acceptance, love and the will to move on.

The Imposter Syndrome

It has happened so many times over the years that I have stopped trying to count. I am on the stage, and I am owning it. I am totally and wholeheartedly in the zone, connecting with my audience, feeling the energy and knowing that each moment I am more alive than the last. Somehow, in some way, I feel almost transported in those moments, as I know I am doing what I have been created to do and it feels so amazing to be alive.

And then I walk off the stage.

I either go behind the curtain or I step to the side, and make my way down. Some days I meet lineups of people, waiting to say thanks, waiting to encourage me or ask questions. It should be the moment when I feel like I totally belong and that I can rest assured that I will know the next step. Instead, I often experience something very different.

I hear the voice, the recording, in the back of my head, asking me those same old questions and reminding me of what I could be tempted to believe. I am somehow, in some way, tempted to feel that I am an imposter. I am not good enough to be able to hold this responsibility. In fact, I half expect the authenticity police are going to bust through the back door at any moment and ask to see my identification. And then, they will out me.

I have wrestled with how to conquer the accusations that shame has continually made to me. Why do I feel this way? I am not lying when I speak or do any kinds of communication. I am not making my facts or stories up and I am definitely not claiming to be someone I am not. Yet I am somehow tempted to believe that I don't deserve to be able to do what I am doing, in that place and that moment. I question whether I deserve to be so happy, connected and alive. Why do any of us wrestle with accepting and validating ourselves when we need it most? There often seems to be a default in many of us to find it easier to resonate with feelings of shame, allowing that story to eclipse our success by telling us we don't deserve the affirmation or the fulfillment that we desire.

Leaning into the Feelings of Shame

Perhaps it's time to stop giving in to shame. Maybe, instead, it's time to lean in.

Don't worry, I am not saying we should make hot chocolate and invite shame to a cuddle party or anything weird like that!

I prefer to liken shame's effects to that of a porcupine quill. Porcupines are a weird part of the landscape in the world that I grew up in. You could find them in the most unlikely places, being lone and solitary little creatures that like to climb trees and sneak across roads and ditches when no one is looking.

And really, who is going to mess with a porcupine anyway, right?

Trixie was our family dog, dubbed a "Heinz 57" because she had no distinguishable features of any single breed. She was a stray puppy that found us and became a member of our family. We loved her fiercely, even with all her quirky ways.

Like every dog, she was curious, and like every dog that lives in the country, that curiosity usually meant that she was tangling with squirrels, skunks, coyotes and porcupines.

Many times throughout her career as the Duncan family dog, Trixie would come home with quills embedded in her nose and face, evidence that she had, yet again, made another porcupine angry. And every time it would break my heart as I listened to her whimper and cry from the pain of the encounter, probably anticipating the greater pain she was yet to experience when we dealt with the removal process.

The curious thing about porcupine quills is how deceiving they are. To the naked eye, they look like they should be no different than a pointy needle, easy in, easy out. But they aren't. When a dog or other animal tries to attack or bite down on a porcupine, it can release its quills in self-defence (a porcupine can have up to 30,000 quills on its body). Like an arrowhead, they slide easily into their attackers, by the dozens or even hundreds. Each individual quill is made up of layer upon layer of hair that has become hard and sharp, and each quill has a deadly secret. The quills have razor-sharp, fine points and because they are surrounded by hundreds of microscopic barbed layers, they are merciless. Once they have made their entry point, they will continue to burrow deeper and deeper into the attacker's flesh, eventually puncturing internal organs and slowly bleeding an animal to death.

I remember how Trixie would howl and cry as we held her down and pulled out the quills with pliers, and I remember how it broke my heart to see her in so much pain. As we pulled out each quill, it would continue to tear her flesh as, with all its barbs, it fought against being removed.

But if we didn't deal with it, it wasn't just about the quills not coming out. It was about the further and deeper damage those quills would continue to do to her as they worked their way deeper into her flesh. Damage that could be prevented while we could see the quills and identify the source. No one wanted to have to deal with it and hurt poor Trixie like that, but there was no other option than to face removing those quills head on.

Shame is like a quill. Shame happens easily when we aren't asking for it, and it burrows deep into each of us. Each tiny, invisible barb has a different source. Sometimes it seems so easy to pretend it doesn't bother us - until we get really and truly honest with ourselves. And due to its nature, shame is willing to lie in hiding, in the dark, as it waits for the opportune time to attach itself to our emotions and our deepest connection to who we are.

It goes after us at our core, and it can seem so innocuous as it just seems to be the way that the world around us works:

We get pointed out in school.

We were picked last for a team.

We spoke our mind and were shot down.

Someone we trusted did something they never should have.

Our house didn't look like everyone else's or our family was a little different.

Teenage hormones wreaked havoc on our skin and made us stand out.

We have a discernible physical disability.

We learned differently than everyone else.

And as if childhood is not enough, we then grow up and our boss, partner or friends point out our mistakes in front of others. We forget the 99 percent that we are doing right and we hear only the 1 percent that resonates with the shame we carry.

The list can go on and on and on because there is no end to our imagination's ability to connect those moments of shame with our feelings of self-worth and identity. Before long, we're identifying ourselves with the shame rather than with anything else that defines us.

I am no stranger to those thoughts. In fact, many of them were mine at some point in time, and they followed me incessantly. There was no way to see it from the outside though, unless you are an expert on picking up on subtle signs. But they were there and they refused to leave me. Like porcupine quills, they went in quickly and easily but their damage was slow and steady. They needed to be dealt with or they would tear away at the very core of who I was.

I fought against them, I pretended they didn't exist, I hid behind doing really great things for others and for the world around me. I stood on stages and in front of crowds and tried to silence the shouting in the back of my head about how I didn't deserve to be there or be given that responsibility, all the while becoming more panicked that someone was going to call my bluff. I will never quite sure what I thought that "bluff" was. Regardless of that fact, the thoughts still existed.

It was time to stop running and to learn to identify the shame at its source, to lean into it by being honest with myself about the path to freedom

Leaning into my shame is not about identifying with it - it's about identifying that it's there in the first place. I can no more stop that nagging feeling of shame than I can stop myself from breathing. It's a part of my history and I am better for recognizing it. The feeling of shame is very real, but it is still just a feeling. We choose whether or not we will accept it as part of who we are.

That subtle distinction is the difference, and that's what it means to lean in.

I don't deserve to be doing what I am doing or standing where I am because I am perfect. I deserve to be there because I have worked hard, I have done the work internally inside of me, and I own this story now. This is what I choose: to be defined by what I am, not what I was or what I was told I should be. I am defined by my decisions and acceptance - nothing else. Nothing that has ever been said or done to me can change who I am.

I am loved.

I am not a mistake.

I belong here.

I am part of a divinely ordained plan.

I am capable of being successful.

I am capable of learning from my mistakes.

I am enough and I have the resources to recognize what I need to do to continue to move forward, and even better, change the world through the process.

The same is true for you.

The Push to Prove

Have you ever felt that awkward need to prove yourself? To prove to someone you love, someone you desperately want to be accepted by, that you are enough for them? You change, you morph, you shift everything, from your values to the way you like your eggs cooked to what they want. All because you aren't enough just the way you are.

Shame motivates us to run from the responsibility of taking ownership of our feelings. It drives us to prove, over and over again that we are good enough. As if by changing all the outward things we are somehow able to magically make the inside match whatever is convenient on the outside.

I have tried that route, over and over again. And that went well for me each time.

For about 5 minutes.

The truth is that there is no way to ever make the outside match the inside. The outside shifts and changes, and is always dependent on circumstances, opportunities, situations, and others around us. The story that we choose inside can become our compass, our rock, the one thing we have control over. Others will perceive us as they want, each one in different ways. Trying to match our self-perception to theirs is a fool's game and, like porcupine quills, will destroy us if we let it.

How Teaching English Taught Me About Dealing with Shame

I have one tried and true method that I have come to make my own when dealing with shame. It's not fancy (nothing effective ever does seem to be fancy, does it?), but it works. I acquired this tactic through the daily quest to teach English to my daughter.

Widlene came into my life at the most inconvenient time possible. I was a mess, and I was convinced that there was no way I could ever not be a screw up as a parent to her. In the background of my life, my marriage was already falling apart and things were out of control. But in the present, I was sitting in this dodgy apartment in a town in Dominican Republic, alone and trying to learn how to connect with this little human who came with a built-in personality, and who wasn't yet quite sure how she felt about me or the future of us being family. To be truthful, the jury was still kind of out for me, too.

Well-meaning people would tell me over and over again that I was going to be a great mom and that it would come naturally. I know they meant well, but it all meant absolutely nothing to me at that point in time. In some weird way, the more I heard it, the less I believed it.

The problem was, I couldn't own a truth that wasn't mine in the first place. People told me that I was a good parent based on what they saw on the outside, but I didn't believe them because I knew what was going on in my head. And what was in my head wasn't pretty in the least. I was confused, worried that I had screwed up this kid's life with this decision and there was a part of me that resented all of it. I didn't know how to adjust to a four-year-old's life. I couldn't even think of another four-year-old that I knew. I felt so ashamed of my thoughts, my fears and my endless screw-ups.

But I leaned in to it. At first, it was because I had no choice. She had no one else and I had made a commitment. But then it became less about doing the right thing and more about giving myself permission to be me.

As Widlene was learning English, she and I would play the point and name game. It was how we communicated in the beginning. I would praise her whenever she used the right word and sentence structure for communicating, and in turn I would watch her flourish under the praise. It was all made possible because objects and ideas became recognizable to her as her language capabilities expanded. Names replaced pointing and her vocabulary and accuracy rapidly increased.

Without names, objects are unrecognizable. There is nothing to distinguish from the clutter of the scenery or the clutter going on around us. As our communication began to flow, my panic eased and I began to see this time for what it was: a gift beyond words.

That time also taught me about how I saw myself and, ultimately, how I began to deal with my own shame at my shortcomings. I saw the pattern between pointing things out and naming them one by one, and how that cleared the air for ease of communication. I began to deal with the shame in my life, one moment at a time.

I realized that I only *felt* like a crappy mother. The truth is that I was learning, I was in an incredibly difficult transition, and I was capable of growing. And later, when my marriage would completely derail, I knew that it wasn't because I wasn't worth loving or that I was an irreversible screw up. I was loved, I was enough and I was going to be okay. I was in an impossible and painful situation. I needed to take responsibility for how I felt about everything, but I was not defined by those feelings.

I refused to believe in shame's twisted stories and fables. Besides, shame never had anything new to say that I hadn't already heard so why bother listening anymore?

I am the hero in my story. I may be a flawed and imperfect hero, but it's still my story.

What stories has shame told you?

Sometimes they come at the witching hour, causing sleep to elude us. The comparisons happen, over and over again. You press play on the button of your shame triggers and it all starts. Conversations are replayed, moments are re-lived, actions are examined over and over again. They roll around in your head, serving as proof to your bruised self-confidence that there is definitely something incredibly wrong with you. The message seems to be all too clear: you are unacceptable.

But let me ask you something. It's a question that I wish I would have been asked a long, long time ago, because I think it could have saved me a lot of wasted time, energy and pain.

What are you ashamed of?

Go ahead, pretend you aren't ashamed of anything. No one is watching, listening or sitting in on your internal dialogue. For many of us, shame has probably been lurking in the shadows since we were old enough to be cognizant of how we felt.

I don't have all the answers, and some of your questions may truthfully need professional counsel and assistance (and might I add, if that is the case, I would say that this question was a success!) and you should feel free to seek that no matter what.

But do you want to free yourself up from a lot of needless weight and encumbrances?

Start shaming shame by putting it out there. Send a video to yourself, write an email to yourself, send it, read it and then delete it.

Do whatever you need to.

But name it.

Name what you feel so ashamed of, what has held you back and what you think is so wrong that you can't see past it. Once it's out there, it's recognizable.

No matter how ugly or menacing it is, name that little sucker so that it can't hide anymore.

Name it so that your life can resonate with the unshakeable feeling of freedom and acceptance.

Name it so you can stop feeling worthless and start knowing you are enough.

Name it so that it's only a minor character in your story - not the whole story of who you are.

Name it so that you can open up to all the possibilities around you and recognize what is good. Doing that will help shed understanding on how you can help to make the world a better place for others.

Your story deserves to resonate with all the ways you have continually, time and again, refused to allow shame to determine who you are.

Tell yourself that story.

And never stop.

Chapter 7

I Could Have Sworn That Was a Gum Ball: Stories of Nailing Toxic Behaviour

I was about three years old. When you are three, the concepts of time, space and boundaries are not very clear or defined in your mind. Your perception is pretty limited to processing whatever is in front of you, giving you the ability to tune out anything else.

Perhaps that was how I came to find myself digging under my grandparents' bathroom sink. Nothing was off limits in my mind and everything was an adventure waiting to happen. Because of that, when I saw them, I couldn't deny my curiosity to find out more. They were the most luscious little pearly-pink gum balls I had ever laid my eyes on, and for some reason they were under my Grandma's bathroom sink.

I knew vaguely in the back of my mind that I wasn't supposed to go digging around in places I had no permission to be in, but the curiosity far outweighed the fleeting thought of repercussions. I wanted to know everything about everything (I still do) and that's probably why when I saw them, I felt entitled to them. I thought about how much other people had been holding out on me, hiding those gum balls under the sink like that, and I knew that I needed to have them for my own.

In a moment of self-righteous indignation, I grabbed a little fistful of them and popped them in my mouth, preparing myself for the luscious bubble-gum taste to squish out. Something squished out, all right, but it wasn't bubble gum. It was bath soap. Yuck.

They weren't gum balls at all; they were bath beads. As I cried bubble-bath tears and burped bubbles, I watched my mom and aunts laugh and try to show empathy for me at the same time. My insides revolted against the slimy liquid in my tummy. The bath beads may have been good for a bubble bath but they were toxic to my digestive system and I quickly found out why!

Lesson learned: there was a reason why I was told to not go snooping under the bathroom sink. And even though my mom knew better when it came to my safety, my curiosity wanted a quick fix. In the end, I had to deal with the bitter results of slimy bubble bath suds burping out of me for hours afterwards.

It doesn't take a chemical genius to recognize that anything that is toxic for us internally needs to be dealt with for our health and future. It's the same for who we are at the very core of our being. We can't truly become the best version of ourselves when we are stuck in what I like to call, "toxic loops": default reactions to life situations that we get stuck in repeating, over and over again. They become our quick fix for feeling better and enable us to feel like we don't have any personal responsibility.

I love quick fixes, don't you? I wish all of life was able to be handled by the Staples "That was Easy" button, and all my emotional turmoil and life challenges could be magically snapped into alignment with my wishes. In fact, whoever invented duct tape was clearly the ultimate lover of the quick fix. There is nothing that duct tape can't fix, from falling car bumpers to keeping electrical cords in place. If only life had a duct tape app to consult.

In many respects, quick fixes are everywhere, from the types of food we eat, to the way we break up long-term relationships by texting or messaging, to how we automatically default to pointing the blame to someone else instead of taking responsibility for something messy. Our default is often the path of least resistance, and I am humbled to say that there are numerous times when I have succumbed to that same path.

Recently, I made the commitment to live a wheat-free life. There was a time when I would have considered being gluten/wheat-free something that was only for desperate celiacs and the odd hard-core organic freak. But not now. I had decided that it was time to take control of my health and I needed to educate myself on what was really the best for myself and my future. That led me to the conclusion that, for me, it meant I had to go wheat-free. (Wheat as we know it is not what it was even 150 years ago, and the GMO version—that is, the genetically modified organism—that we have today in everything from flour to "healthy" whole wheat is causing great concern over what it is doing to our bodies. GMO wheat has been linked to many diseases and disorders, everything from diabetes to brain function. So for me, the only answer was to remove it completely from my diet. It really did change a lot of physical things for me that I don't want to lose out on ever again. For more information and how to do it in a healthy way, check out the book *Wheat Belly*, by William Davis.)

The blogs and literature that I read warned me that, as with any other addiction, I would experience a few days of adjustment and needed to learn how to navigate the cravings that were created by my wheat addiction. They were right. I didn't feel like a heroin addict, but I could definitely tell that I was going to have to make consistent, conscientious choices every day about what I was going to eat. It wasn't just going to be about running out to Whole Foods and buying up every item labelled "gluten free" on the shelves, as there are still lots of gluten-free items that are not the best choice for me. (Bacon, anyone?) It meant stopping a cycle that was a default for me. Starbucks gingerbread cookies were a comfort food that I had to be honest with myself about because I had a bigger picture in mind for myself - not a bigger waistline.

Recognizing toxicity in my life and relationships wasn't so different from letting go of wheat. First I had to be in agreement that I needed to change, and that the responsibility was on my shoulders to decide how to do that. And then, I had to do it. I wanted to change the story around the toxic behaviours in my life, so I committed to making that happen, one decisive step at a time.

That's So Unfair!

It's so easy to see the patterns, faults and flaws of others, don't you think? Whether or not we care to admit it, we like to use ourselves as the standard by which we measure everyone else. There is a part of us that is convinced that our views, our experiences and our perspectives are the only true ones to consider in a situation. We can easily convince ourselves that what we have experienced is the only true side to the situation and the only true way to evaluate what's happening. Sometimes we will even go to great lengths to try to convince others of our version of the situation, trying to manipulate and pull them over to our side of the story.

When something is physically toxic, it can harm us or even kill us. One look under the sink will tell you what you should be careful around (besides bath beads). Items that are toxic or corrosive to our physical health are clearly labeled with scary warnings to be extremely careful in how we handle the item.

But the difficult things about emotions and relationships is that they don't come with those same labels. When we fall into our own bad habits and defaults, there is no little skull with lines through it to warn us that we are headed down a path that will only continue to harm us and diminish our future possibilities. Small levels of toxicity are tolerable for a while, but eventually they will reach critical mass.

Me a Complainer? Why Does Everyone Say That?

I know complainers and I don't like being around them, and I definitely don't want to get into a conversation with them. Had you asked me if I was one of them I would have vehemently said, "No way!" because I refused to see myself as one of "those people": the kind of people who always seem to complain about everything and everyone.

They seem so innocuous at first, those little complaints. And before you know it, they become routine. I think back to how easy it was to begin complaining about others' actions, about how difficult life was getting, about how I felt so judged, so disregarded, so rejected. Like a sinister arachnid, complaining pulled me deeper and deeper into its web of toxicity. My complaints started out with what I told myself about how sad and unjust everything was, but they soon spilled over into finding new people to tell them to.

I am cringing as I type these words out on my screen, because I know they are true.

Let me clarify something here: my pain, like yours, was very real. There is no denying that the situation was incredibly difficult and at times it was unfair and uncalled for. But complaining didn't serve to change it, and it definitely didn't serve to change me for the better in the middle of it all. In fact, complaining put me on a toxic loop of focusing only on what was wrong with everyone and everything else — and it convinced me that I had nothing to do with the outcomes.

I had to change that pattern.

I remember when I decided that I was the only one who could make it happen. It was as if I finally heard what I was saying from someone on the outside, and it wasn't pretty. This had to change! I needed to start somehow, in some way to change my perspective from one of complaining to one of finding what's right in the situation. I made the decision to start with finding five things at the beginning of the day to be grateful for that day, no strings attached. It would have been easy to focus on being grateful for air and freedom and other default settings, but I wasn't going to let myself off that easily. Gratefulness had to be about changing my perspective and about recognizing the possibility in the circumstances. Finding gratefulness in challenges pushed me to be more creative with my problem solving, and finding gratefulness in my physical freedom reminded me of all the opportunities that same freedom gave me to speak up for others. Gratefulness is a powerful character habit that changes us over and over again.

So the next day I made myself do it again because I didn't want to miss out on the benefits it offered. I still do it to this day. Every single morning, as I am waking up, I list off five things I am grateful for.

And like letting go of wheat to be physically healthier, replacing complaining with gratitude is becoming my default now. Focusing on the positive rather than the negative helps me get a better perspective and realize that there will always be things I want and I can't have; but there is way more to life that I can experience and embrace, if I am willing to be grateful for it all. Every time I choose not to be "toxic," I win, and so do the people around me. And so does the future that I am building for myself. I need to choose who I am going to be, because no one else will do it for me.

Do you wonder if you need to change this aspect of your life? Here's a little test: ask three people around you how often they hear you complain. Brace yourself for the answer!

I Would Trust You, Except I Won't.

We each have lenses or filters with which we approach life. Many of them are just natural bents that we can't necessarily change such as our desire for connection or our need to have things in an orderly fashion. But one filter that we can choose to change, to help stop a toxic loop in our lives, is the filter we use with trust.

When we have been hurt, we tend to park on how that hurt happened and the memories surrounding it all. It can be a cultural or racial issue, a gender issue, an intimate trust that was broken, or even something we confessed in confidence that we later found out was not kept that way. However it happened, trust was broken in our past and it can be hard to want to trust again. When we feel that, we look for other people who feel the same way. It often seems that like attracts like.

This is a toxic way to build relationships and it can never turn out well for us.

Relationships built on a mutual dislike for someone or something are incapable of leaving any room for real growth. For example, you have a friend that, every time you get together, you complain about work, about the opposite sex, about your family or partners, about anything that is outside of you. Is that relationship really going to be someone who you could build trust with? Are you someone they could feel the same about?

The truth is that we can easily fool ourselves into believing that the other person or the system is always the problem, never us. It allows us to feel self-righteous and justified in finding fault, and in finding someone else who feels the same way as us. Warning: run from that as fast as your little legs will take you. Toxic is as toxic does. It can only ever produce its own kind.

We each have lenses on life, but the difference is in how we manage them. Acknowledging that we have them can lift judgment and help build relationships of depth and trust. Giving in to them and believing that our experience is the entire spectrum of possibility can damage our judgments and perspective. And in the end, we are the ones who lose out on understanding others through not understanding ourselves.

It's Totally Your Fault!

The blame game is this little game I used to like to play. For a while it was really fun and entertaining because it helped me feel like everything was okay with me. Essentially the game revolves around a single concept: I am okay, you are not okay.

The blame game is easy to play: you can play with one to one million people and all you need to have is something to point at. Roll the dice and let the games begin.

To play successfully, you need to make many, many assumptions. Make them generously and let them run rampant in order to gain blame-game points.

Assume others are wrong, they are selfish, they are going to hurt you, they are judgemental, they are thinking something bad about you, they are talking behind your back, they are not listening to you and they will never understand how hard life is for you.

Blame generously, blame often, blame without discretion. Rinse, repeat.

The blame game is the worst game every invented. And yet everyone still keeps on buying into it because it is always the cheapest game to play and it always gives immediate gratification - for a time.

And then it will come back around and bite you in the butt.

But be warned: they don't put those labels on the packaging. That's how they get you.

I finally threw the game away. Its novelty ran out and blaming others is exhausting; the opportunities will always be endless to engage in it. Sometimes I find little left-over pieces from the Blame Game under furniture in my head and heart, and I just toss them out with the trash. That's where they belong.

Get Ready, it's Time For A Detox!

Detoxification rarely brings about immediate gratification. Our systems have grown dependent on the path of least resistance and it can be hard to re-orientate ourselves in the beginning. Detoxing brings up many challenges. By its very nature, it can seem counter-intuitive: although you acknowledge that it's good for you in the long run, you know it's going to be forcing you into some uncomfortable states of being.

You can get headaches, diarrhea, and shaky moments when you are on a physical detox. As you rid your body of the toxins that have been building up, you're doing something that's painful in the moment so that there will be rewards for the long term. Unbeknownst to you, those toxins could be causing you great harm in the tiny little spaces inside of you. And those tiny spaces, left unchecked, could grow into bigger spaces that can destroy your body with relentless, malicious intent.

Detoxing who you are is not a whole lot different. It can be kind of painful when you first start out. You may feel disoriented as you aren't used to taking a certain route in your thought processes and emotions. The default circuitry wants to run the show and a power struggle may ensue.

It's okay. I've been there.

I still have to revisit it often, to be honest.

For me, it started with one word: forgive.

Yes, I just said that.

Sorry, it had to be said.

I know, I know. They did some really brutal things. There is no denying that what they did or said to you was cruel, wrong, or [insert other painful adjective here] and doesn't deserve to be forgiven. The one obvious exception to this is abuse, as there is never an excuse for it. There is no situation in which we should ever feel we need to protect someone's reputation if they have committed physical or sexual abuse. It is not only wrong, it's a criminal offence.

But the only way to stop the toxic loop of resentment and anger in *you* is to forgive. And then, you just keep choosing forgiveness every day after that, until you create a new loop for yourself. You forgive for your own sake, not theirs. You only live inside of your own skin; they will have to deal with their own actions.

And forgiveness will give you something in return. It will give you inexplicable, beautiful lightness of being. The kind of lightness that gives you ease and generates an energy inside of you that you didn't know you were capable of possessing.

Think of all the energy your anger is taking up, and think of all that you could do with that extra energy! You could probably train for an ironman triathlon with the energy that it has taken to stay angry! There are so many ways that our default button for anger can try to suck our energy and focus. But perhaps there is more to the frustrations of life than meets the eye.

It wasn't the "stupid cops." You were speeding.

It wasn't the difficult person who made you rage like a lunatic; you allowed yourself to get frustrated. No one makes us frustrated; we choose that state of being for ourselves.

It isn't your crazy friends who suck you into partying and being reckless; it's your decision to not care enough to stop.

It isn't that he's a jerk or she's catty; it's what you decide about who you are that changes things.

God isn't conspiring against you. It rains on the just and the unjust. Don't think that just because you have good intentions it means that God has to bless whatever you want. (FYI: this one was particularly hard for me to let go of!)

Maybe the people around you aren't all negative - maybe you are.

Try to go just *one* day without pointing a finger. See how it feels. Then try it again and again and again. And don't stop.

Toxic Relationships that Needed to Stop

There will always remain the possibility of extreme levels of pain and hurt threatening to alter the course of our lives forever. One of those is when we have experienced being betrayed by someone we have loved and trusted. Someone whom we thought was on the same team as us, in the same understanding as us, or even willing to look out for our best interests. Someone whom we thought would always put others ahead of themselves and would certainly never break their commitment or word. Experiencing betrayal truly feels like a knife cutting through your back, tearing your core as it descends. It can leave you breathless, as though the wind is knocked out of your lungs and you have forgotten how to breathe. The people at the centre of my relationship circle betrayed my trust, and I became so focused on what was messed up within the relationships and the absurdity of what was going on that I became like a frantic, drowning person. I was thrashing around, trying to hang on to anything that made sense, anything that could help with bringing my world back into a recognizable state.

But you have to remind yourself that you know how to breathe, that your life is going to move on and that above all, you are going to be okay.

It kind of started like any other detox program I have tried for my health. I got panicked that I wouldn't make it through the next few hours without the defaults that I had grown so dependent on. Only this wasn't wheat, chocolate or any other form of food, this was me at my very core. I had to draw out the poison, moment by moment, to be grateful, to forgive - even though I didn't feel it yet. Without reminding yourself that there can be life beyond the pain, you will get caught in the rut of toxic communication, where you continue with blame, distrust and resentment. But you can never give up and park there. That only results in toxic relationships that lose all levels of health and security. You have to choose to move forward in spite of how you feel.

The landscape of my life had completely changed, and I was in a new and unfamiliar place. I needed to get back in the driver's seat and learn how to navigate in this new place. It started with a re-orientation, like learning to drive on the opposite side of the road when you travel. I had to make each move cautiously, reminding myself to reverse the process that would be the automatic default in the place that I used to live in when I felt victimized and powerless and without hope. I needed to adjust to what it would take to be safe in this new place of opportunity, of hope, of new beginnings.

What Toxic Stories are Resonating with You?

I didn't write this book to preach at you. I wrote it to share my story, because stories are what we remember, what we will come back to time and again. It's humbling to be honest and authentic about where I have come from and about the toxicity I allowed into my heart and mind. But the freedom makes it worth it all.

What toxic stories are you allowing to resonate in your life? Forgiveness can seem so impossible and at times it can even feel like admitting defeat. Blame is easier to default to and easier to hide behind than taking responsibility. But that's a toxic loop of avoidance and it never ends well.

There is a common phrase in the world of speakers and those of us who step on the stage: "Fake it 'til you make it." The declaration isn't about being fake or giving false pretenses — it's about what you focus on when the spotlight is on you. It's about giving yourself the freedom simply to be, to try a new way of being on, until that new way becomes your new normal. Similarly, taking steps to leave the old loops behind and write your own story can probably feel a bit like you're faking it at first. But if you keep trying, you will soon find your own, new voice and be able to write your new narrative.

Forgiveness and responsibility are like that. We forgive for our own freedom, nothing else. Forgiveness isn't necessarily a heartwarming or joy-inducing decision, either. Many times, when it comes to forgiveness, I have had to fake it until I made it. I chose to forgive before I felt like I truly owned the feeling. And each moment and opportunity that I had to choose it, I would choose it over again. In many situations, I have had to move into it and act on the concept long before my feelings ever matched up with truly forgiving someone. But choosing forgiveness stopped the toxic thoughts and actions, and that's the first step.

I decided that I definitely needed to take responsibility, accountability and even my fair share of blame for the history behind me. Some of that responsibility was even in how I had allowed myself to be treated. I was worth more and I always will be. In the regular failures, fiascos and train wrecks of life, we just need to admit where we went wrong, even if part of that admittance is about how we have devalued ourselves and our worth.

When we allow ourselves to be treated a certain way, even though we know we deserve better, we rob the world of the gift of the most authentic version of us. Because of that, forgiveness often has to start by looking in the mirror, owning how we have treated ourselves, and forgiving ourselves for withholding respect from the person looking back at us. It's a heartbreakingly beautiful place to begin.

And the person looking back from my mirror is really quite amazing. I am looking forward to a long life of getting to know her better.

I wish the same for you and the person staring back from your mirror.

Chapter 8

Questions to Ask When Standing in Broken Glass: Stories of Discombobulation

It happened so fast that I didn't even see it coming. One minute I was focusing on making sure I didn't stall my car as I simultaneously worked the gas pedal and the newly installed clutch. My light turned green and I moved forward into the middle of the intersection.

After that, all I remember is bouncing off the light pole on the opposite side of the intersection. I didn't see him coming and I didn't hear him because he didn't even have time to stomp down on his brakes or honk his horn. He only knew I was there when he was a millisecond away from plowing into me at 60 km/hour in the late summer twilight.

There must have been a loud crash as brakes squealed and metal crunched against metal, shattering all the glass attached to it as both cars moved together in an altered trajectory across the intersection. When I came to a stop, I crawled across the front seats hastily and jumped out of the passenger side door. I started walking around, staring straight ahead. I was in shock and I couldn't figure out how I came to be standing beside my squished up, bright yellow ancient Pontiac Sunbird. The man who hit me came running towards me and just kept saying over and over again, "I couldn't see you. The sun was directly in my eyes. It's not my fault."

I didn't even care what he was rambling on and on about. In fact, I didn't even know what I cared about in that moment. I was in too much shock over how quickly everything had just changed.

Someone must have called 911 immediately, because the police officer seemed to come from nowhere. He began asking me questions, but as he started talking to me, I couldn't process what he was saying or asking. All I could focus on was that I knew him because he had just married a girl from the ward that I volunteered on at the local hospital. So instead of answering any of his questions, as I stood there in the middle of broken glass, with blood trickling down the side of my head, I calmly asked the attending officer how his recent honeymoon was.

He began to laugh and said, "It was great, but I think you should maybe sit down for a minute, okay?"

I was clearly not in my right frame of mind and I was trying to figure out which way was up in my current situation — and the feeling was kind of foreign to me. I was grasping to be normal and feel in control, but I couldn't focus on anything that felt familiar. I was babbling and the only person I had fooled into believing that I was in control was myself.

I was clearly discombobulated.

Discombobulation is one of those words that paints a vivid and accurate picture as you say it. It's the perfect word that never gets enough airplay in our vocabulary.

When you are discombobulated you don't know which way is up. The familiar stabilizers in life elude you. You can't figure out how you ever got to where you are and you have no idea how you can ever put things back together.

In other words, the ass just fell out of your life!

The Beginning of the End

Years later, after my bizarre conversation with my friend the policeman about his honeymoon, I found myself standing in front of a crooked, white pedestal sink in a dodgy hotel in northern Haiti, one breath away from a meltdown.

I was there because I needed to find some answers about how to proceed with the adoption of my daughter and I could only get them in person at the embassy in the capital, Port-Au-Prince. That particular day had started early, shortly after sunrise. I piled into a small, rented SUV with five friends and headed to the Haitian border. The plan was that three of us would get out at the border, catch the bus into Cap-Haïtien and fly the next day down into the capital, returning the following day after I had a couple of meetings and found out some information that I couldn't get over the phone.

Two hours into the trip the truck started smoking. And then it started coughing. And then, with one final shudder, it gave up the ghost, leaving us on the side of the road in the middle of nowhere, with a dead truck, no water and no cell service.

As the Caribbean sun got hotter and hotter, our patience grew thinner and thinner as we tried to figure out what to do with the truck and the conundrum of getting to the border before it closed. As we sat there waiting, a truck full of local workers came chugging along, and to us they seemed to appear like a desert mirage.

We decided to split up, two going with the truck to return it to the rental agency and three of us carrying on towards the border, in hopes of catching the bus there. As we flagged down a small, overcrowded mini-bus in the desert frontier of Dominican Republic, I felt I had no choice but to hop on and hope for the best.

It was nothing if not entertaining!

As we careened around corners and sped on straight highway strips, the bus driver was equally generous with both the accelerator and the brake. Because of this special skill, I began to notice that every time the driver slammed on the brakes, feathers floated up and I could hear a squawk from under our seat. Finally my curiosity got the best of me. Leaning forward and looking under my seat, I noticed two chickens being held upside down, in the hands of the lady next to me. As I stared in disbelief, she politely smiled and nodded. I politely smiled back and swallowed down the urge to gag at the smothering smell of feathers and chicken poop in the overheated and cramped space.

Four hours later, after a harrowing border crossing experience, I found myself reaching out to take a room key from the owner of a hotel in Cap-Haitien. At first I couldn't tell we had pulled up to a hotel, as there were no signs or discernible pictures, and when we walked in, there was a family sitting around eating chicken and rice while watching a small TV. The man stood up and shook my hand and said welcome, leading me to another bare cement room with a rickety desk and low-hanging light bulb. As he fished around in the desk for a pen to get us to sign our check-in receipts, I couldn't help but notice the fact that the entire lower level of this hotel was raw cement blocks, with bare bulbs hanging in what seemed to be a random order.

We walked up the uneven, winding stairs and down an unlit hallway. He opened my room first, and it was the most welcome thing I had seen all day. It had a single bed, a small, ancient TV on a console, and a separate door for the bathroom. I smiled politely and said thank you to my host.

As I heard him leading my friend down the hallway to his room, I realized just how tired and overwhelmed I felt. The stress of the day swelled up and threatened to make me cry. I walked into the bathroom to wash my face and clean up at the sink.

Standing over the sink, I began to retrace my steps from the day and realized just how far out of my element I truly felt. I was scared and overwhelmed by something that I couldn't wrap my mind around, something that was happening just below the surface in my marriage and my life. An unknown future and the stress of the present situation preyed on my every thought.

I leaned in to wash my face and noticed a long, black hair in the overflow hole of the sink, about three inches away from my nose. Strange, I thought. I never noticed that hair there a second ago. But then that long, black hair twitched, and revealed that it was actually the antennae from a massive, black cockroach that almost stuck its head into my nose. I had no choice: I had a royal meltdown.

Screaming, I ran from the bathroom and leaped across the small room onto the rickety bed, causing it to shimmy and shake, as I shook on top of it and burst into tears. They weren't polite, heartwarming tears, either. They were the kind of tears that wash away mascara in a heartbeat, make snot flow uncontrollably and somehow even make your hair into a tangled mess. They were tears of shock, stress and discombobulation.

They were the tears of the soundtrack of my life at that moment, and I could no longer stop them from flowing. I had lost the will to bother trying. I didn't know which way was up anymore, and I knew that I had reached my limit.

And so it began.

Over the following months I would often feel like I was watching my life unravel just beyond my grasp. I felt the panic of not knowing what was secure, not knowing how I ended up there or how it would all end. In those dark days, when everything further unraveled with each passing day, I felt more and more disconnected and discombobulated. I don't even know if the details matter anymore. Details can be limiting in their scope and they can sometimes cloud the bigger picture. Details as to why we hurt, why we are angry, why we lash out, or why we struggle with moving on eventually begin to fade. If we let them, those details begin to diminish in importance. Not because what happened wasn't important, because it was. But when we are in the middle of what can sometimes feel like compounding crises it can be hard to find our anchor point. It can be hard to connect back with feeling like we are still in control when all outward indicators seem to point to the contrary.

But here is where we can use feeling discombobulated to our advantage: we can actually realize that we will never totally control the situation – but we can always, always control who we are. Life will never wait for our permission, but we can always take every chance we get to choose who we are and what we become as a result.

Questions at 6:00 a.m.

Less than a year after my tangle with that cockroach, I was standing out on the street in my underwear, sobbing and screaming for someone to help me. It was 6:00 a.m. and the sun had not yet risen on the north coast of Dominican Republic where I now called home. I am pretty sure I woke up an entire community with my screams.

I had fallen asleep on the couch the night before. I was alone in a big apartment on the second floor. Sometime just before sunrise, I could hear rustling at the kitchen table, about 15 feet away from me. In my foggy half-awake state, I rolled over to face the kitchen and bolted upright as I realized there was a man standing at my kitchen table, holding a machete and going through my belongings.

I screamed. I don't think I meant to, it was just the first thing that went through my mind and out my mouth. I screamed and I screamed, and I didn't stop. Even as he turned towards me and ran at me, holding up the machete, I couldn't stop screaming.

I screamed for the guard, for a neighbour, for any kind of help I could stir up.

I don't know what the common human reaction is in moments like that, but in my shock and disbelief at what was going on, I felt as if my brain suddenly split in half, with one side telling me to shut up and give him whatever he wanted, and the other side saying don't stop screaming.

I listened to the screamer.

In hindsight, that might have been the very thing that saved my life.

My attacker didn't expect me to scream, and in his panic at my incessant noise, he stopped waving the machete at my face and grabbed my laptop and iPhone which were on the coffee table in front of me. Spinning around to leave, he made a move to run through the patio door beside me. Only the window was closed and he actually bounced off of it!

As I was screaming and watching this whole scene unfold, my brain was still divided over what to do. I remember thinking that the incident with the patio door was really funny, but I was also gravely aware of how close I had come to being in mortal danger, I just kept screaming and didn't give up.

I have no idea how I even found the key to get out of my front gate, but the next thing I remember was standing in the street outside my house in my underwear, crying and screaming, and in shock that I could have just been killed by a man with a machete in my living room.

Somehow, deep down inside, I knew that everything as I knew it from that point forward, was over. This episode was about more than a man with a machete, it was about the end of a marriage and a long, painful struggle with trying to make sense of everything that was happening without my permission in my life. The realization of the crisis of being in physical, mortal danger somehow opened my eyes to the magnitude of crisis in my life in general. I had reached the point of no return in my emotions, in my relationships and in what I was willing to tolerate in myself anymore. I was tired of trying things that weren't working, tired of trying to be someone I no longer could maintain, and tired of feeling like I was powerless in my own life.

I was at the peak, but in some way, when we reach those points in our lives, there is a sense of release in knowing that something is over. Even if we didn't want to let it go, doing so creates space inside of us to reach out and pick up hope again. Being at the peak of crisis eventually has to result in resolution. Depending on how we want to see it, that point can become an end to something, or it can become a whole new beginning.

Why It Can Be Hard to Let Go of Crisis

We are a culture that revels in thrills. They make good stories and give us the sense that we have experienced something exciting and memorable — and perhaps we have. There's absolutely nothing wrong with the desire for excitement and memorable experiences.

But crisis can also leave us craving the next rush, whether it is physical or emotional. We love the highs and lows because they are what make us feel so alive.

Discombobulation can be like that. We can develop an addiction to the drama of the next bad thing that is happening, similar to the thrill of the roller coaster or watching an epic movie or drama series. Jumping from one crisis to another, whether real or contrived, can be a rush.

We get accustomed to whatever we keep on experiencing, whether it is good or bad. We create those bad-habit loops again and again for ourselves and those loops can cloud our ability to judge where we truly are emotionally and the value that we bring to the world. They happen to the best of us, no matter where we come from, how much money we make, or how many people love us or hate us.

We can get hooked on drama, crises, destructive thoughts, being driven to seek approval, questioning our value in each and every situation, looking for an excuse as to why we say or do certain things. We can even get so comfortable in crisis that we don't know how to re-orient ourselves back to normal, whatever normal really is.

One of the surprising things I realized about myself was that I had somehow become hooked on crisis. I never thought it would happen, but it did. The truth is that, to a certain degree, every crisis was somehow exciting. And even though it was destructive, it made for a wild ride.

But it truly is a ride I don't ever wish to repeat.

I would like to introduce you to my new flame. His name is consistency, and let me tell you, he can light you up like nobody's business.

There was a time when I was scared of consistency. I am not naturally wired to be attracted to the slow and steady things in life. I am wired for sound, for experience, for adventure. I thought that I would never be able to truly love consistency because it seemed to be the opposite of adventure and excitement. But I now know better.

Consistency has way less to do with what we see (externally) and way more to do with what we feel and experience (internally). To limit consistency to the physical impression is to miss the subtle, stunning, powerful force that consistency brings to our lives and the universe around us. Consistency can't be cheapened and shortened down to something that we do or say. Consistency is about the very fiber of what we have been created to be. (Brace yourself, this might rock your world!)

Consistency is the very fabric of what life is made of and it is the very essence of the universe around us. The state of being consistent doesn't mean you are predictable and stuck in a rut - it means you act in line with your very nature.

Consistency opens the way for true resonance in our lives because everything will connect with that with which it shares the same nature. Small, consistent acts of kindness are what empowers the bigger acts to have more effect. Small, consistent thought patterns that remind us of all the potential inside of us lead to us resonating with a bigger story of confidence and commitment to work things out.

Consistency is beautiful and secure. And it can be the story we tell ourselves over and over again: the story of being in true alignment with our deepest values, no matter what life throws our way.

If your very nature is to value relationships and connection, then you will always be drawn to act consistently with that nature. If your essence is to crave adventure and wide open spaces, you will always have the default setting to act, live and move in line with that nature. If you are a visionary and drawn to continually dreaming, exploring and creating new possibilities, you will always, always be pulled toward that nature. It is what makes life, existence, seeking and consciousness beautiful, affirming and life giving. We have been created, birthed and shaped to be consistent and to live our lives in alignment with what we value at the core of who we are. That alignment creates a peace like no other we will ever know. It's a beautiful, irrevocable gift that is ours to embrace.

When we feel disoriented in who we are and where we are going, we aren't being consistent with our nature and with the order of things that we exist within. The peace we seek will elude us unless we embrace who we are and what we know we truly need and want. Embracing our true essence, and acting consistently with it, gives us grace — for both ourselves and everyone else in our world.

Consistency is one of the most beautiful things about being fully human because it gives us permission and creates space for us to resonate with who we are at our core.

And that's how we begin to change the story we tell ourselves when we feel discombobulated and disoriented in our lives. When shame, disappointment, and toxic defaults tempt us to let our guard down and to lose sight of where we are going, consistency and alignment can bring us back, every single time. We ask ourselves what we will do, how we will move forward and where we will go based on who we have been created to be all along. We ask ourselves what story we want to resonate with - not what we want to react to or fight against.

There is no striving or need for motivation when we come into alignment with our essence and truest nature. There is only grace and peace there because it's home for us. And once you get there, it's the only place you will ever want to hang out.

When my life systematically fell apart all around me, I was left with two options: give in to the hopelessness and remain in the chaos and panic OR find my true north. Truthfully, it wasn't even a matter of choice, just a question of where to begin and what I was willing to do to make it happen.

One day I held a conference with me, myself and I (the travel logistics were a killer). As I called the meeting to order, I laid out the ground rules. We were collectively here to decide the direction that we were taking, and we wouldn't be returning to this place ever again.

I was the only one who knew these answers, yet I had refused to seek them out until things had reached the point of no return.

Here is what I asked myself:

What was important to me? Why?

How did I want to feel about who I was? Why?

Where did I want my life to go? Why did I feel that was the best direction for me?

What was I not willing to compromise on from this point forward? Why?

Who was I going to be in the middle of this - no matter what would happen in the days ahead?

As I grew more and more honest with myself, a pattern began emerging in my findings. Looking back over my life and my panicky approach, I realized that I had been spending my energy in the wrong areas. I had been trying to control everything outside of me: my relationships, my situation, Live Different, Widlene, but the truth is that the only person, place or thing in it all that I could completely control was me. I had been looking outside of myself for so long and believing that if I just worked hard enough, loved hard enough and controlled hard enough I would eventually get everything to acquiesce to what I wanted it to be.

That approach had clearly not served me well! If I was to find my way back out of this maze into the daylight again, I was going to have to stop some very destructive patterns.

First, I was going to have to stop believing and telling myself over and over again that my life was out of control. (Sound familiar?) Every time we say our lives are out of control, we can't do it, or it is impossible, whether we acknowledge it or not, we begin to identify with those words, because we continue to believe them more and more. Our words create worlds through the power of the social architecture we build around them. Consequently, the only way to change our behaviour is to change the way we think.

Every debt specialist will tell you that one of the biggest indicators of whether someone will get out of debt and stay out of debt is the way that they view their power in the situations they find themselves in. Those who verbalize and consequently camp their understanding around the tenet that they have no control in the situation will inevitably end up back in debt. In line with the consistency of our thoughts and actions, without there being a shift in how they think and act, they will return to that situation.

The same goes for every single area of our lives that we live out on this earth. It starts with changing the way that we think.

How do you feel about discombobulation?

Who knows? Losing control may actually be what you come to be grateful for!

In fact, the apex point of discombobulation is not really about losing control, even though that's what it may look like on the outside. But to see only that would be to miss out on what the true peak of profound disorientation really is.

Losing control and the re-orientation that can happen because of it is actually about the creation of an opportunity.

The opportunity to gain control back in what *really* matters.

The control of who you are going to become.

That new, true control comes in the form of being consistent with who you are, what your values are, and in keeping your gaze on who you are choosing to be.

It's not easy, but it's not as complicated as we make it out to be, either.

It starts with being willing to ask questions of ourselves and being brave enough to answer them honestly.

So here's to all those crazy encounters in life that shake us to our core: to the chickens on buses, the cockroaches in hotel rooms, the half-crazed machete-wielding neighbours, the thoughts that steal our peace and make us wonder if there is more to life.

Here's to misunderstandings that we need to navigate, to unforeseen crises that show us what we are made of and to the people who push us to the edge and beyond.

Here's to unplanned parenthood, relationship train wrecks and suicidal career choices that left us empty inside because they were never meant for us in the first place.

And here's to the financial crises that make us rethink what is the most valuable to us and what legacy we want to leave behind.

Thank you for shaking us up, dumping us upside down and giving us the chance to reflect upon our own values. As a result, we are presented with the opportunity to choose to be consistent in our choices and character — and we can now understand what we are capable of becoming.

Thanks to discombobulation, consistency is able to show up—if we are willing to let it in. And when it shows up, it's there to remind us of something we sometimes forget along the way...

About how incredible this life is if we are willing to embrace it for what it is and what it can become—what we can become.

Quite frankly, discombobulation might just be one of the best things that ever happens to us!

Chapter 9

Falling in Love: Finding Dignity in Recognition

"We look for what we want, but we find what we believe. " Mark Rayner

One of the first creatures I remember from my childhood is our family dog, Parky. I vaguely remember him for a few reasons. One of those reasons is a faint scar on my chest from a lesson learned: do not pull the dog's tail.

When I was about five years old, Parky disappeared. My dad told me that he went into the forest and never came back. I believed the little white lie hook, line and sinker; I had no reason to doubt it. In my formative young mind, that dog had just wandered away into the forest beside my house. Naïvely, I hung onto the hope of him one day wandering back out to play again. I never questioned this version of reality until I was a late teenager, and one day I had a random moment of clarity and realized that all this time, my dad didn't know how to tell me he had to put Parky down! Realizing that Parky didn't abandon me was somehow a sense of relief and closure for me over 15 years later.

Moments of recognition are hard to define. For example, as small children, how do we ever begin to identify that a dog is a dog? Somehow, in some mysterious way our brain makes a connection and from a very formative time in our lives, our brain begins to perceive that every time we see, hear or touch a dog, we begin to identify it as such.

How did that happen? How did we magically know that both a massive German Shepherd and a miniature Poodle are dogs? How did we not think that a cow and a dog were the same because they both had four legs, a tail, two ears and hair?

Perhaps, for me, it was the familiar feel of the hair on the dog's back that I would pet or the way that every dog instinctively tries to sniff and lick at a child's face. It's possible that it could have been about the smell or sound of the panting or barking. Perhaps it was something more otherworldly, something that was beyond what I could see or feel with my senses. Maybe it was about a kinship, a deep connection of trust.

I don't know how I knew what a dog was. The truth is that I just knew.

We somehow learn what something is and why it is so. We recognize that we need to remember certain details about a situation, that we will have to learn to share (even though nothing in us may want to), that there are things in life that will make us feel good and things that will make us feel bad.

Perhaps one of the greatest mysteries about being human is that we have the innate ability to learn from our mistakes, even though we aren't necessarily able to pinpoint what we need to learn at the time.

If you put a baby on a couch and allow him to move about freely, he will eventually fall off (which is not recommended by the author as a psychological experiment, by the way!). As a result, that tiny little human will instinctively know that something about the previous situation caused him pain and harm. He can't make an algebraic equation out of it at this point in his life, but there was definitely something that brought it on. Of that, he is sure. However, because the baby's view of the world is only beginning to take shape, he may not put the two things together that are necessary for him to correctly ascertain the situation and recognize the possibility in the future.

Perhaps in his innocent and malleable memory, he will equate the couch with causing the fall. That may have been the most tactile memory or thought he has around his situation. It's possible that he might blame the blanket that he thought would keep him safe no matter what. Maybe it will be the sounds in the room at the time or even the presence of someone else that he will associate with the experience. He might not initially be able to attach the idea that his own movements brought him to the edge of the couch or to the fact that shortly thereafter he fell to the unforgiving floor 16 inches below. The only thing that he might grab on to in those initial attempts at interacting with the world around him is that there is something in the experience that he needs to remember for future reference.

Love is like that for me (only much more beautiful than falling from a couch!). Every time I fall in love, whether it has been with my partner, my child, my career, a culture or group, or new ideas, there is something in that initial encounter that reminds me why I feel love for it. It looks a little different every time, but at the core it's the same. It fills me with a knowing, a peace, an excitement for what is ahead — and an unstoppable desire to have more of it.

That's why I knew I couldn't not let go of that first time I met Widlene. There was nothing cinematic or romantic in that first encounter, just that familiar little flip of recognition in the very centre of my being.

The village she is from is a beautiful, chaotic, heartbreaking and tangled mess snugged against the backside of a hill, on the north coast of Dominican Republic. Within that community there is love and hate, birth and death, loyalty and betrayal, heartbreak and elation. Ultimately, it is a community like millions of others around the globe, full of imperfect people doing their best with the life they have been given. People like you and me.

I wasn't the first one in my group to encounter her that day. Numerous friends that joined us as we visited that village would tell me about the famous little "Snot Ball," this sassy little toddler who teased them, followed them around giving them attitude, and who had a perpetually runny nose. I didn't know her, but I felt like I knew her all of my life from the first moment I held her in my arms.

Even though she smeared her nose on my shirt as she squirmed to get down!

I loved her spunk and tenacity but didn't even think any more about it. Her mom was standing right there, and we were having a stilted and awkward conversation in my limited Spanish about her life, her family and the community.

I still look at pictures of her mother and wonder if she knew who I would become when we talked on that hard dirt path between crowded houses. As we had talked that day nosey neighbours listened in and I was continually feeling the pull of so many little hands on my clothing, jockeying for the attention of the visitor.

At the time, I was new to understanding the implications of involvement with humanitarian projects on every scale, how my heart would swell and then be crushed, and how it would raise the flag of hope again and inevitably be torn out and trampled on many times over.

But I knew that feeling that was growing inside of me. The seed of new love that was fragile yet determined to put down roots and name its new home. I thought it was s simple affection for a kid that I connected with and made not much more of it.

I left shortly after that encounter with Widlene and her mother and went back to Canada. I moved on with life, not really giving it much thought as I was once again caught up in the flurry of life in my world. There were bills to pay, messes to be straightened out, vision to continue pushing forward. And then there came a phone call with a sad update.

Truthfully, even when I heard that Widlene's mother had died suddenly, my first thought was not about adoption. It was only about how sad it was that she was left behind. I thought of all the children in that village and around the world that had drawn the wrong numbers in the birth lottery and the sheer enormity of it felt much more acute to me because of my attachment to one little life. I hoped someone would help her out, not once questioning if I knew any "someones" who might be able to help.

One evening, everything changed.

It was a crisp, spring evening. I had been in a hot yoga class and was just savouring the last remnants of the heat and clarity that I felt after such a great practice as I walked home mulling over the next steps in life. My thoughts turned to Widlene, as I hadn't heard anything for a long time. I began to wonder how she was doing and what became of her — if someone had ever helped her family. And then, seemingly out of nowhere, the little voice that I knew asked me a valid question.

"What if you are that someone?"

I hadn't ever asked myself that question before, but on that sidewalk in my sweaty yoga gear, I knew I recognized the answer. I knew that I was that someone. I knew I had to find out more.

Within a nanosecond, I had another thought: What the heck am I thinking? There is nothing I can do and, quite frankly, my life is full enough without complicating it in the pursuit of a kid I know nothing about. And besides, I told myself, I am clueless about parenthood and my life is messy enough as it is.

I really wanted to listen to the second stream of thoughts. They were so appealing, so plentiful, so seductive. They seemed so safe. I could have listened to them, reminding myself that I really didn't know if I wanted kids in the first place, that I had enough to worry about with the rest of my life, and even that it didn't make any financial sense (and I had enough financial crises to last me a lifetime anyways).

But recognition showed me something else. Recognition showed me that I wanted this more than anything. Even though I felt nauseous at how much work it would take (I didn't even know the half!) and I felt totally insecure at what kind of parent I would make, I couldn't stop the seed that was acknowledged inside of my heart for the first time. I knew what love felt like. This felt like something that could turn into love.

But I didn't know where to start. There are some things in life that are overwhelming purely because you have no previous experience to hold them up against. You feel completely out of your depth and don't even know how to identify or verbalize what you want to see happen. You just know you are too far in to turn back and you have to keep moving forward.

My heart and soul were now inexplicably connected to this little life thousands of miles away and I couldn't will it to stop or turn from this longing, no matter how hard I tried. I thought of her constantly, wondering how I would ever find her or get an answer to the questions that loomed inside of me. Questions about whether I could ever be capable of raising her properly, if I was good enough to be a parent, and even if I would be able to figure my own life out enough to make room for her.

Two months after I made the decision to pursue adoption, I was back in Widlene's village — only now I was sitting across from her grandmother. As I nervously looked at her, I was taking her facial features into account. Widlene had her eyes, she had the same feet in her worn out flip flops as Widlene's and her head tilted to the same angle as she weighed out what was being said. I knew beyond the shadow of a doubt that my life would never be the same and we would be tied together by a little life that didn't understand anything about what was about to rock all of our worlds.

But as I sat there, I also recognized something else. It was the familiar sense of commonalities. As I stared with hope and trepidation at this woman across from me who held the power to take my request into consideration or not, there was more we had in common than we had separating us.

We both knew loss.

We both wondered if we could trust each other.

We both wanted the best for this child.

We both had no idea how complicated the whole thing would get.

Somehow, knowing that we had way more in common than we had differences helped me to feel that I had a partner in this plan and that we would be able to figure something out, together.

Because we were now connected.

Connection is a craving within the human experience. To a certain degree, I think we all long to feel connected, even though it may look different for each of us.

When you travel, if you find someone from your area of the world, it's easy to automatically feel a connection of location.

When you have experienced a type of suffering or loss, there is often an easy connection with someone else who has walked through a similar experience. Connection can even be built on a similar taste in cultural or lifestyle choice that we discover in someone we barely knew beforehand.

Connections can be as significant as finding commonalities over our relationship struggles or as simple as a common love for a certain type of car, genre of music, designer or restaurant. It can also be found in the truth behind "opposites attract" when we realize how easy it can be for us to connect with someone who is the opposite of us in so many ways, yet seems to complement our views and needs.

Connection gives us the ability to process and understand how we feel about ourselves and our world because it helps to lift judgment. When we feel a connection to someone, we want to try to understand them better. Ultimately, connection gives us the ability to tap into a simple yet deeply foundational aspect of who we are and how we connect.

Connection helps to point us towards dignity.

Everyone has a picture in their mind when they hear the word, dignity. Perhaps it's of a little old lady with a puritan-like bun on her head and Victorian-era clothing, walking with a straight spine and masked expression on her face.

Maybe we envision someone who is facing death with an acceptance and grace that shakes us to our core as we question whether we are capable of the same. It could possibly be as simple as the kind treatment that some are capable of giving to the vulnerable and exploited regardless of who they are or where they find themselves.

For me, dignity has come to be about the power of recognition.

If I am willing to look close enough, I can see a little bit of me in everyone I meet. I see it in their hopes and dreams, and in their values and aspirations. In the end, we want the same foundational truths to be present in our lives. We want to leave a mark on the earth and have a sense of significance.

On my first trip taking volunteers to Dominican Republic with Live Different, I met a woman at a garbage dump. I will never know her name and I will probably never see her again, but I can never forget how she gave me a sense of recognition. As strange as it may sound, in her I saw a glimpse of who I wanted to become.

We had brought hot meals to the hundred-plus people that were working there that day. Like anywhere else on earth, each person there had a story to tell. I didn't ask her about hers and she didn't volunteer any information. However, as I watched her come forward to accept the meal I held out, I was profoundly touched by how beautiful she was. She was physically beautiful and carried herself with grace and presence and the girl inside of me was kind of jealous at how she managed to do it. But she had something more than that. As she sat back down on the side of a pile of garbage to eat her meal, I noticed that she ate delicately and with intention. She had the unmistakable presence of quiet confidence and that confidence made me want to be around her, to know her and to be in her presence just a little while longer. She carefully and thoughtfully chewed each bite and when she was only half way through, she discreetly packed up the rest of the food to take home later, probably to a household of lives that depended on her.

Almost ten years later, I can still remember her face and how she sat there. In fact, in many ways, I have used it as a measuring stick for myself in many different circumstances since then.

Meeting her made me realize that dignity had to start with me. I had to be willing to acknowledge what I needed (not necessarily what I wanted) before I could understand how other people deserved to be treated.

There is dignity in choosing to do a job well done, no matter what it is. (Fast-food fry-guys, unite!)

There is dignity is knowing when to fight back and when to bow out.

There is dignity is being free of the compulsion to prove myself or my worth, in knowing that my true worth isn't dependent on what happens or what other people do.

There is dignity in not putting someone else down to make myself feel better.

There is dignity in looking myself in the eye and acknowledging my faults — and celebrating my strengths.

There is also dignity in doing it for others.

There is dignity in being able to protect other people's names and reputations - whether they deserve it or not according to our subjective view of justice.

There is dignity in knowing what you want and not settling for less.

There is also dignity in not yet knowing, but not panicking and living helter-skelter in an effort to uncover it.

There is dignity in choosing to become a voice for someone whose voice has been shut down, silenced, or ignored.

And above all, there is dignity in recognizing who you are and what you are capable of doing.

Dignity is about recognizing that I am connected to others. How I view them and treat them is a reflection of how I truly feel about who I am.

The Tattoo That Changed my World

And so that's how I came to darken the door of a dodgy little tattoo parlour in Pattaya, Thailand. I was there because I had decided that I would get my first (and probably my last) tattoo.

We had just finished up a long and fulfilling two weeks with our first team of volunteers in Thailand with Live Different. For the first time in my life I had laughed and cried with a group of survivors. I found out how the victims of slavery have faces, names, dreams and struggles that can be very similar to mine. I had played, laughed and had seen with my own eyes the incredible power of resilience and hope. I would never be the same.

On our last night in the country, we went south to a city outside of Bangkok called Pattaya. It must have been beautiful at one time, nestled along the bay in a lush and inviting area. But now it only seemed to me to have the hollow exterior of a façade that is desperately trying to hide something far more sinister and destructive. Something that insatiably devours hopes, dreams, and freedom itself. It's a false front for a merciless trade in exploitation of human flesh: slavery.

It's hard to describe what that walk that night came to mean to me but it started with a suggestion from some local people who ran the children's home we were helping that day. They told us that the best way to understand what Pattaya was about was to visit an area called, The Mile.

The Mile is a long, busy walking street built around tourism, mostly foreigners looking for sex. It is a typical market street in some ways with everything from fast-food stands to knock-off purses, but there is so much more. It's also filled with endless bars, karaoke clubs, coffee shops, and dance clubs that are all outlets to sell sex from. And sex is available to anyone— anything they want, for whatever they are willing to pay.

But it's not the Pretty Woman scenario of free will and true love. It's a place of stolen childhoods, traumatic loss and devastating memories — all smoothed over with a smile and a bow. It's a pervert's paradise.

At first, as we walked down The Mile, it seemed surreal — as if we were in some kind of alternate reality where there were no consequences for anyone's actions and the goal was to take what you can get. In many ways, perhaps that's what it is for many people who visit that area. But for those of us together on that team that night, it was devastating to see where kids like the ones we had worked with can end up without the help of intervention and love.

Somewhere along that street we saw a McDonald's sign and decided that we needed to get inside for a moment to process it all. I waited outside on the step for everyone. I was leaning against the hand railing and trying to absorb what I was seeing in front of me. This was a place without shame and it seemed so overwhelming to think about how it could ever change.

I am ashamed that I felt that way, yet I know that I am not alone. It's uncomfortable to feel pain for others, and it's easier to convince ourselves that we have enough in our own lives to deal with.

But Mother Teresa was right. She was once asked how she handled all of the pain and injustice that she saw and her response was beautiful and heartbreakingly eloquent,

> *"I have found the paradox that when you love until it hurts, there can be no more hurt, only love."*

I am no Mother Teresa, but that night something changed for me and it came from an unlikely source: a flower I had never before held in my hand. I smelled something very beautiful around me as I stood there on those steps. Perhaps the wind changed. Perhaps I just began to wake up to the environment around me and that touched something inside of me that I was ready to recognize. I will never know. But that night, in the middle of one of the dirtiest places in the world, I smelled one of the sweetest fragrances possible.

I was standing underneath a plumeria (frangipani) tree and as the breeze wafted through the branches, the flowers gave off a beautiful and gentle scent.

I picked one and held it to my nose, marveling at how something so beautiful can live and thrive in a place that is so ugly in so many ways.

And I thought of something that I have told countless students, countless times. Bullying and violence happen in countless locations around the world because there are three groups involved: the bully, the victim and those who stand around and watch it happen without intervening. Their silence becomes their consent to allow it to continue. Perhaps they are scared it could be them next, perhaps they are too self-absorbed to get involved, or perhaps they are paralyzed by their own shame.

But there is no shame in dignity. Dignity is about identifying with that other person and realizing that we need each other and deserve to be treated as equals in the relationship.

My silence would become my shame if I didn't begin to get vocal about what I had seen and experienced. My silence would become my shame if I didn't decide to honour who I was by honouring those around me.

My silence would be my consent that it was okay for others to be exploited, sometimes even for my gain.

I had to make a decision. I had to open my heart to the recognition in me that this was the only way to honour myself and the space I hold in this world. It wasn't about feeling guilty, it wasn't about being charitable or a good person. It was actually about recognizing who I am before I can do anything else.

I am worth more than consenting to the ill treatment of others. I am worth more than pretending I am little and powerless to change things. I am worth more than not acknowledging that their dreams and mine are both beautiful and deserve to come to pass.

As I held that flower that night I realized that exploitation doesn't continue simply because evil is so powerful and exploitation is so unstoppable. No, it exists because evil is so convinced of its power and exploitation has determined that it will be unstoppable.

What would happen if we each became convinced of the unstoppable power of love and mercy instead — and we decided to pursue it consistently, intentionally and unashamedly, with every decision and step we took?

It's not a call to arms. It's not a call to perfection. It's not a call to shout from a soap box. It's an invitation to change the way you think about the power you possess — the power to *be* love and mercy in this world.

That was a moment in my life where eternity collided with the temporal place I found myself. It altered my view of the power I truly had to effect change and I knew that I couldn't live my life any other way. It was an epiphany.

So as I held that little flower to my nose and waited for the group to come back out, I looked around for something to make it real, something that would always remind me of the influence I am capable of having -- that I could play a huge part in changing the world around me. My eyes landed on a blinking sign that said, "We use clean needles." It was a snap decision but I don't regret it at all.

Yep, I got a tattoo in the redlight district of Pattaya, Thailand. It hurt so good.

I decided it would be the plumeria flower and underneath it, the Thai translation of Jeremiah 29:11, the very same scripture that I found in my brother's Bible so many years earlier.

"For I know the plans I have for you, says the Lord. Plans to prosper you and not to harm you. Plans to give you a future and a hope."

I had three different sets of eyes confirm that the translation was correct before it was final, because I wasn't about to go through all of this and end up with a tattoo that was pretty but said something deep and intelligent such as "spring roll" in Thai that the artist thought would be funny.

As I got that tattoo, leaning over a chair on the second floor that looked out over the pedestrian street below, I watched a foreign man approach and start talking to two girls in their mid-teens standing outside the entrance to a bar. He stood there talking to them for a minute and suddenly a little boy came out and clung to one of the girls' legs. She was a working mom and judging by everything I saw, she had been doing this for a long time. Long before it would have been a choice of free will. I watched as they talked for a moment and then she grabbed the man's hand and they walked into the bar, out of sight.

That girl may have looked free to make the decision to sell herself into that life, but chances were she had ended up there from someplace far, far away and there was an even greater chance that she ended up there because she was sold long before she was able to understand what was even happening to her.

While the tattoo gun hummed in the background and made permanent imprints on my lower right side, I made a decision for myself. The decision that I would remember who I am so that I can become a voice for who others are as well. And every time I look over my shoulder at the mirror, I remember why I made that decision that night.

That decision is ultimately what drove me to find Widlene and dig into my courage to hang on when everything grew more and more difficult in every area of my life. That decision was what started me on the truest path to freedom, as I recognized what I was capable of doing, and who I was capable of becoming. That decision changed my life because it changed my mind on what my story could be about. My story could be about all that I have come through and learned, and that would bring a certain measure of value. But the resonance in my life, and yours, comes when our story points the way to dignity and hope, both in ourselves and others.

Dignity and hope are free to give and own, but they are not cheap. They sometimes come at a high cost. That cost is different for each of us, but it will inevitably involve changing the way we think about ourselves and our connection to the world around us. It is about using our voice and actions no matter what is required because we are all connected.

Recognizing our common needs, goals and potential is not only proof of our humanity, it's proof of our value.

I wanted answers and quick fixes, but what I needed was to recognize that the only thing I can truly control is who I am and how that understanding connects me with everyone around me. Dignity is truly about how we treat ourselves first and how that points the way to how to treat others.

Understanding How Your Voice Carries Resonance

Being honest with others is often easier than being honest with ourselves. As I type these words, I am tempted to think of all the times I have fallen short of the ideals I have set out for myself. I am tempted to count and re-count all the disappointments, the failures, and the words and actions I wish I could take back.

But I can't. And neither can you.

And somehow, knowing that and recognizing who we can become in spite of all of that is what makes our lives that much more authentic, more real, more beautiful.

It's what reminds us that there is dignity in how we take those experiences, memories and encounters and weave them into one incredibly beautiful story of who we really are and what is yet to be discovered. From the smallest of encounters to the larger than life memories, the resonance continues within us in whatever way we choose.

What story will you choose?

Chapter 10:

The Kryptonite Chronicles

Clark Kent could easily be perceived as the ideal man. He's both steely and sensitive, the ultimate hero. The perceived underdog, his true power and strength remain hidden from the world. The world sees only what he wants them to see — in fact, they see only what *they* want to see.

Of course we know that underneath that Clark Kent, underdog exterior there is Superman, the man who overcomes everything, the man of steel. He may have come from another planet the rest of us don't understand, but he is just like all of us. He is flawed and he has a weakness.

For Superman, his weakness comes from somewhere far in his past. It represents something that many of his kind before him were unable to overcome. It even followed him to earth, lurking and waiting for its grand entrance.

Kryptonite.

No matter how far he goes or how hard he tries to convince himself he is unstoppable, he will never completely escape the power of kryptonite. He will always have to navigate around it.

We all seem to have our own personal form of kryptonite in our lives. I never used to see it for what it was; however, it has been a part of me for so long that I had difficulty identifying it at first. It followed me down the halls of my school, to every job and career choice I have ever made, to every relationship I have ever been in. Sometimes it came in such close proximity to me that I felt weakened and unable to stand on my own. At other times it would linger, far away in the background, with only the odd flitter on the air waves around me, sending a subtle, yet persistent, reminder that it hasn't forgotten about me.

I avoided my kryptonite for a long time because I didn't understand it. I could see its shadow in things that I would do and say, but I never wanted to take the time to sit down and really be honest about its hold on my life. And because I pretended it wasn't there, in the dark recesses of my mind and heart, I could go on like nothing was wrong, tell myself I was okay, tell myself that I would figure it out someday, but not today.

And then I would start the cycle again. Coming to every experience, every encounter, pretending it wasn't there, hoping that it would leave me alone. Hoping it would give me reprieve.

But Kryptonite doesn't have to pursue you. It just has to remind you that it exists and that's enough for you to know you need to be careful.

Meet My Kryptonite

It's actually quite painful to vomit it out for the first time for the world to see. But after you do, it gets easier, you walk with a humility and the power that comes from that humility. You wonder what took you so long to just 'fess up.

So here's my confession, my personal kryptonite (and I am willing to guess that you won't be much surprised by the time you have read this far into this book!): All of my life, I have wrestled with the question, the lingering doubt, that I was never, ever going to be enough.

That I would never be good enough at anything I set out to do, to hold someone in a relationship, to accomplish what I truly wanted to accomplish with all that is within me. It's played out in so many ways over the years that I navigated around it without question. But that underlying doubt will never fully go away. Like kryptonite, it will always be around and will always be sitting there ready to wreak havoc in my life if I choose to allow it.

For a long time, I let my kryptonite kick my butt. Every experience seemed to remind me of why I wasn't enough. The range was as broad as childhood hurts and disappointments to a failed adoption and marriage, and as subtle as convincing myself I was unable to learn anything technical or detailed because I wasn't capable of grasping those kinds of concepts. I have stayed up at night worrying about public perceptions about my life and the judgements that I became convinced were happening.

All because my weakness has always been that one question.

Am I enough?

But I have found that I am just going to have to come to terms with this question every single time it corners me in my life. And the answer is that I am enough because I am here. And I will have to choose to believe the answer over and over again.

I guess you could say I have come to realize that I walk with a limp. And I am totally okay with that.

In the Bible, Jacob was a man who "wrestled with the angel of God." As a result, his hip got zapped in the encounter and for the rest of his life, he walked with a limp. His name got changed as a result, but so did his gait. Everyone limps in life when they get into a tangle with the biggest questions that haunt them. When we face our kryptonite we recognize that it's where our weakness exists, and that can be a scary place to search out. But just because we have a weakness doesn't mean we are weak or that we are defined by that weakness.

In fact, it doesn't mean that at all.

Never trust someone without a Limp

Everyone limps from their tangles with kryptonite, but not everyone wants to admit it. Some of our scars are outward: physical limitations; the results of disease, accidents, maltreatment by other people; poverty. And some of them are inside: brokenness, betrayal, wounds that have gone on for years, childhood trauma.

Everyone walks with a limp, but not all of us are willing to embrace it and move on from it. Some of us want to pretend that the limp doesn't exist, that we can keep it hidden forever, that we are invincible and unmovable. But when you wrestle with the questions about your weaknesses, and have the courage to ask yourself who you really are when you aren't pretending, the story might be very different. Because now you are walking with a discernible limp. And I don't know if you have received the memo yet, but limps are the safest thing you can carry around with you. They remind you that acknowledging the limitations doesn't mean weakness, it means that you have found a different way to tap into your strengths and to work around the limitations.

Somewhere along the way I decided to stop pretending that my kryptonite wasn't a part of my story. It's like denying you have a child the moment you give birth — it just doesn't work in the real world. It exists and so do I, so we need to establish who is going to determine how this will play out.

I was tired of all the guesswork of trying to placate my insecurities and still trying to grow. It could never work. So, I decided to change the relationship I had with my version of kryptonite by learning how to accommodate walking with a limp.

One night, a stranger showed up...

One night Forgiveness showed up at my door, inviting me to take a long, romantic walk on the beach at sunset.

"No pressure, we don't need to be lovers right now, we can just be friends. Even acquaintances. You can just get to know me a little bit," Forgiveness said. (In my mind, being a hot-blooded heterosexual woman, Forgiveness is a tall, dark-haired Latino, but whatever turns your crank).

As Forgiveness invited me to get comfortable, I thought, "Okay, I could do that. It can't hurt to at least be friends and listen to what you have to say. It's not like you are asking to move in just yet."

But he was a very sly companion. We started to have more conversations. He would push me, asking me why I couldn't forgive the people who had hurt me, why I couldn't forgive myself. I pushed back.

We did this weird tango thing for a while, with me always dragging behind him across the dance floor. But it got exhausting. I ran out of excuses, I ran out of reasons to point a finger.

I eventually began to give in to all of Forgiveness's flirtatious suggestions.

And then, Forgiveness and I tied the knot. It was a quiet affair, just the two of us, but it was what I heard other people tell me about. It was beautiful.

It still is.

Forgiveness didn't negate what happened in the past. Forgiveness was unable to re-write history, justify it, or reposition the blame. It just made me realize that my limp is okay, and that I am who I am partly because of it.

I can't change that I have an emotional limp and why I do; I can't control others; so I choose who I am every day. Without knowing it at the time, when I was starting to entertain the idea of hooking up with forgiveness, I was learning about grace and understanding of others.

I had a long list of people I needed to forgive, but the first place I had to start was with myself. I had blamed myself for so many things, all because I was convinced that I wasn't enough to overcome it all. As I began to choose forgiveness, over and over again, without even realizing it, I began to not be so hard on myself.

I had been hurt a lot by other people. In fact, mostly by well-meaning people. It wasn't like I showed up in the middle-school playground every day for 30 years and was chased and beaten up by bullies. But because I was hurting and unwilling to embrace who I could be, every time a criticism came, a word that could have sharpened me or freed me, I allowed it to resonate at a frequency in my heart that was connected to my insecurity.

Forgiveness helped me to understand how to change all that because it gave me the grace to recognize that other people are just as human as I am.

Navigating the Unexpected

When we start out on a new journey in our lives, we have no idea how it will end. How can we? The future is still left to be shaped and formed. It will always look different than what we expected or imagined, but that doesn't mean it won't turn out well in the end.

I never really had much time to share the experience of full-time parenthood with a significant other. My marriage unraveled rather quickly and I found myself on the quick track to becoming a full time single parent, half of the time. I traveled consistently back and forth between Canada and Dominican Republic in order to make ends meet and spend as much time as possible with my daughter and keep her world as stable as possible.

When you become a parent, you will suddenly realize things that freak you out that you never considered before. You drive differently, you talk differently, you are much more careful in so many ways. One of the things you are careful about is how you approach the topic of sex. It is enough to fill anyone with fear and trembling! So when Widlene decided that she needed to know about this mystery, as fate would have it, it happened at the most awkward time of all.

It was a Saturday evening and we were talking to my parents on Skype. Widlene was colouring at the coffee table in front of the laptop, singing her heart out to "Old MacDonald Had a Farm" with my dad strumming along on the guitar from the other side of the world. As they were singing away, Widlene stopped mid-song and said, "Gwampa, can I ask you something?"

My Dad leaned into the screen.

"Sure, what is it?"

"Gwampa, where do babies come from?"

There was a rare, awkward silence followed by the sound of my dad giggling like a little girl.

"Well, ask your Mom."

I silently raged against my Dad as I thought, "I am not going to deal with this right now! I need time to prepare!" So, I hung my dad out to dry and didn't say anything at all, just pretended that I didn't hear what was going on.

"No, Gwampa, you tell me," she persisted.

Now there was more giggling from my dad and then, in a moment of panic, he used the classic deflection line.

"I guess the stork brings them!" he blurted out as he frantically started to play the guitar again.

They resumed singing "Old MacDonald" for a few seconds and then Widlene stopped once more and looked my dad square in the face.

"I think you're lying to me, Gwampa!"

All I could hear was my dad giggling again and pretending he didn't hear her. I finally and mercifully gave my dad an out by leaning in and promising Widlene we would talk about her questions soon.

But in order to do that talk the right way, I felt that I needed back-up support, so I went into the library the next week when I was in Canada. I bee-lined directly to the help desk in the library and asked the librarian what I could use. Her face lit up and she quickly replied, "I have got the perfect book for you!"

The title? *It's NOT The Stork!*

So when I returned back from Canada to Dominican Republic to be with Widlene the following weekend, I gave myself a pep talk in preparation for how we were going to read this book. The book is actually really great, except it uses all the technical terms. I agree with using the proper terms, but in our particular family unit, when you are six and English is your third language, somehow technical names like "fallopian tubes" don't mean a lot to you.

Nevertheless, we walked through the book, talked about sex and all the changes in our bodies, and even about good touch/bad touch. I felt much better equipped to deal with this sensitive topic from that point on. But when my computer rang with a Skype call a few hours later, I had forgotten about Widlene's probing questions for my dad in their conversation a few weeks before.

As Widlene opened up the window on my laptop and my dad's face appeared on the screen, the first words out of her mouth were, "Gwampa, do you have a penis? I have a Jajina!"

And then the next rapid-fire question was, "Do you have sex with Gwamma?"

I leaned into the screen and said, "Please don't answer that!" as my dad, yet again, giggled like a little girl.

That story has a lot of significance for me because it makes me laugh every time I picture my dad's face when his six-year-old granddaughter asked him the ultimate question. It also reminds me of how it opened up the way for a much more significant question that had to be dealt with.

That book and conversation was actually how my former husband and I talked to Widlene about the fact that everything was going to look very different from then on for our family. It gave us the opportunity to help her ask questions and get familiar with the idea that we were no longer going to be a family in the same capacity but that how we felt about her would never change. It was a difficult conversation filled with mixed emotions, but it was one that helped her feel safe. The most important part of that whole conversation became about making sure that the story Widlene would remember was one of being loved and feeling secure — no matter what.

The Comedy of Errors became a part of the journey of intentional love for a child that deserved to always know the security that comes from being loved and safe. And although I didn't want to ever have to have that conversation that way, I have come to realize that by empowering myself to face everything, I was also empowering her to know that we can always decide who we will become.

There are limitless possibilities in what lies ahead for each of us. Why fight it, why look over our shoulder, why pretend we can't be a partner in our future rather than a victim?

There is potential in each of us to live our lives with passion, purpose, authenticity and deep, deep fulfillment. It's what was intended for us all along.

I have learned that even though I was an accidental and totally unprepared mom, I like what kind of mom I am — not because I cook good meals (dear Lord, no one will ever be accused of craving my cooking!) or because I am the ideal soccer mom (I hate mini-vans). But I choose to believe that I am good at this whole thing because I am willing to grow with it, and I am going to live my life in light of that choice.

I am capable of having an incredibly fulfilling relationship and many friendships. I have chosen to learn from what I missed seeing and embracing before.

Above all, I am going to choose to have grace for those things in my life now. I sow grace because I know I am going to need it, over and over again for (hopefully) decades and decades to come.

Our moments and experiences may have scarred us and left us with a limp, but they don't need to be amplified, over and over again. Our stories are full of so much more than the dark, the ugly and the disappointing. Each of us is a partner in the future we are building with the hands of destiny. We co-create it with our thoughts, our words and our intentions. We are not left powerless — we are incredibly powerful!

These are the stories that I will resonate with, because these are the stories that count.

They are stories that are filled with the beauty of our human existence, our connection to what gives us meaning and the power to help reveal our greatest purpose.

And this is where it begins.

Here is What I Know Now

Not a lot! (I wanted to leave a blank page here and freak you out, but thought it would be a waste of energy or a sliver from a tree).

But the truth is, in some ways, the more I know, the less I know about the world, about eternity, about humanity.

I do know that I will *never* again choose to be defined or immortalized by my ugliest moments — even though there have been many. I am defined by the incredible, unstoppable power of being able to choose, every day, who I want to become.

And I want to be the most incredible version of me that the world will ever see.

I want to resonate with stories of hope and grace with more confidence and power every single day.

That's the story that I will tell myself and never stop.

I wish the same for you.

Epilogue:

Perhaps Tomorrow Will Be Our Day

In the northernmost part of Thailand there is a little tract of land that has changed my life and the lives of many others. I have been changed because of the people I have met there, worked alongside of and learned endless lessons about life and love from. Others have been changed because of one person's dream.

By far, the person I have learned the most from is my dear friend and personal hero, Kru Nam. It is hard to put into words the evolution that I have seen over my years of working there and partnering with her and the team, but they are re-writing futures as you read these words.

Kru Nam is from a middle-class Thai family in Bangkok. Her life was one of relative physical comfort and ease, like many middle-class families all over the world. Upon completing her art degree, she moved to Chiang Mai, in the northern part of the country. She was a jewelry designer and she loved what she was able to create. It gave her pleasure and a sense of satisfaction to make beautiful things that would be celebrated. But one day, while waiting for the bus, she saw something that would re-write the course of her life, taking her into places and situations that she never even dreamed of, and leading her down a path to more pain and fulfillment than she could have ever foreseen.

A child was digging through the garbage beside her as she stood there waiting. And as she watched that child, she realized that she had never noticed this part of life around her before. She asked herself, "How could I not have seen this before? How could I have missed that this was happening?"

Those questions led her on a quest that eventually brought her to discover all the kids out on the streets of the city late at night, running around and hustling tourists while their mothers worked in the bars and brothels in the sex tourism industry. It was a world that was as foreign to her as if she would have stepped off a plane on the other side of the world, and it was right there in front of her in her own country.

As her understanding of what was happening just behind the façade of life in the city began to deepen and grow, she felt that she had to be a part of making a difference, and she began with the only thing she knew how to do. She decided right there and then to give the kids a measure of safety and reprieve from the harshness of the streets by offering them art classes. She wanted to give them an outlet through which to connect, but what they gave her was mind blowing. When she invited them to express themselves through art and creativity, they began to draw pictures of violence, pain, and exploitation, telling their story in the only way they knew how.

And this revelation led Kru Nam to seek out people to help her understand what to do, and to determine what others were doing for these children. The answer was that there was very little being done, if anything at all. She had her answer, and she had the resolve to begin to do something, anything to change this situation.

Trafficking in Thailand is a mysterious and horrifying reality. Women and children are trafficked there from Myanmar, Laos, Vietnam, Cambodia and even China, mostly for the purposes of sexual exploitation. It is a vile and horrifying underworld fueled by greed, cruelty, a lust for power and even desperation.

Kru Nam had a choice, and even though no one forced her to make it, her choice was a resolute and extreme one. It was the choice to drop everything and find a way to get kids out of the hands of traffickers and into a safety net that gave them a future.

By the time I found Kru Nam in Thailand, she and the team she had quickly pulled together were already up to their eyeballs with kids that they had rescued and taken in. There were more than 50 of them living in a small, cramped space, surviving together and finding healing. As word spread, help began to show up and Kru Nam's strategy began to fall into place as they found land and opened up their doors to more kids and even young mothers escaping trafficking and the sex trade. They currently have about 130 children at their primary location.

While Kru Nam's actions may sound heroic and even romantic to some of us, many of the people that could have helped make a difference didn't see it that way. Thailand has many different ethnic groups and tribes, and the Thai government doesn't necessarily recognize those people as citizens, leaving them in a cycle of statelessness, poverty and exploitation. Each of the kids in the home is from those people groups. Therefore, finding a place for all of them to go to school proved to be more challenging than anyone had anticipated. No one wanted stateless street kids in their school, yet the only way for those kids to gain Thai citizenship and identities was through the education system, as they would be granted citizenship upon graduation. The very thing that could give them a future was also that which they were denied.

One day, Kru Nam decided that she would take the kids directly to the school in their area, thinking that there was no way a director could turn down a truck full of kids desperate to go to school. She dressed them all in the required uniforms ahead of time, did their hair in the Thai fashion, and did her best to make them look as "Thai" as possible.

They pulled up to the school, and she told all the children to wait outside while she went in to talk to the director, hoping to appeal to his higher values. But what she got was a firm, "no way" from the director. In fact, he wasn't even open to discussing it further and asked her to leave immediately with all of the kids.

As she walked back to the truck, preparing herself to face the kids, she had a choice to make. It was a subtle decision that you or I might have missed if we weren't looking for it. She had every reason to be angry, bitter and enraged at the injustice that life kept on dealing out to her and these kids. She could have yelled at the director, shamed him in front of his staff, or even, at the least, bad mouthed him to all the children when she got back to the truck. But she didn't. In that moment she made a decision that was foundational in what would happen in the years to come.

She stood up tall, walked back outside to all the expectant faces, and without a hint of anger or hatred for the director, she said to the kids, "It looks like today is not our day. Maybe tomorrow will be our day. We will make this work somehow."

In that moment, she became the person for those kids that she wanted them to become. With those simple words and actions, Kru Nam managed to help those kids cut off the default perception of pain, injustice and helplessness before it could even take root inside of them.

It's one of the purest examples of mentoring and leadership that I have ever seen or heard,

They had every reason to be bitter, angry and have a hate-on for the world around them. They had been abused, exploited, traumatized and rejected. But in her wisdom, Kru Nam knew that to give in to how she felt would only perpetuate the cycle of helplessness for her and those kids, and they all deserved something better. They deserved to know what it is to choose, no matter what, who you are going to become. They deserved to stop the cycle of victimization in whatever way they could.

I have never forgotten watching the tears run down her face when she shared that story with us. Those words might have cost her something in that moment, but they became the foundation for how their world has evolved into a place of safety, acceptance and healing.

Kru Nam later found schools for all those children, and many of them are leaders in those schools, winning awards of excellence and achievement, even being exemplified for their character and growth. The possible toxicity was stopped before it ever had a chance to do damage to those young lives.

That's how powerful the stories that we tell ourselves can become. They resonate within us and around us through the lives we encounter, love and hope for. They shape and change the world in which we live because we are changed by what we decide to believe.

You and I are the only ones who decide what we will do with those stories. We hold the power to make them strong, hopeful and beautiful.

And perhaps the most awe inspiring facet of it all is that what we choose doesn't just change our lives in the here and now, it can bring hope and change through the echoes of the lives that we live and move among.

What we choose to resonate with can ultimately become the legacy of who we are.

May our legacies be ones of love, hope and freedom.

Always.

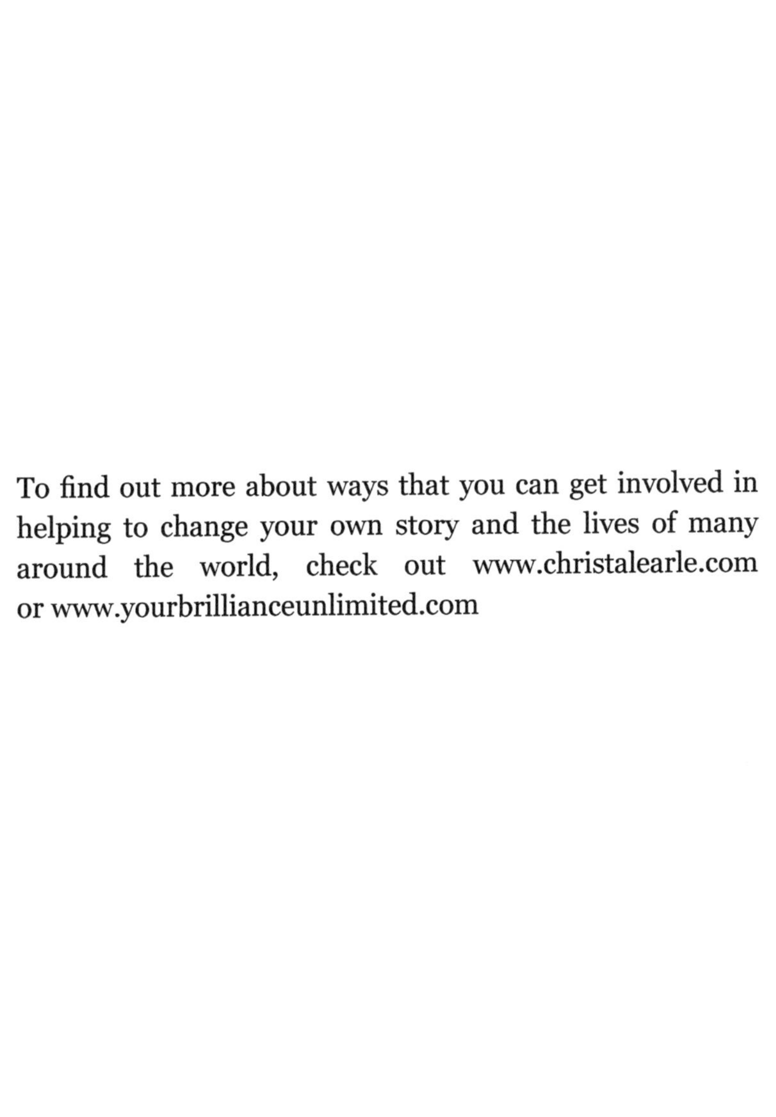

To find out more about ways that you can get involved in helping to change your own story and the lives of many around the world, check out www.christalearle.com or www.yourbrillianceunlimited.com

Acknowledgements

This book was in me a long time before I could get the courage to commit to anything. Perhaps it is like that for anyone who feels the pull to step into something new. Once I did, I found that the most amazing thing began to happen: I was able to find the words, the connections, the thoughts of how to make it take on shape and form. However, there were many people along the way to whom I owe a deep debt of gratitude.

First of all, there were many people throughout our crowdfunding campaign that were instrumental in making the production of this book in your hands possible. People that surprised and humbled me with their kindness and generosity. Thank you for believing in me, but more importantly, thank you for believing in the message of this book. I would like to especially thank Cheryl Treliving and The Boston Pizza Foundation, Rich and Sandra Weber, Andrea Klippenstine and the crew at Live Different. I would also like to thank Karen Milner, my original editor who was very gracious when working with me with deadlines and all that good stuff.

Angela Cacciavilleni has been the spark of genius behind the book campaign and all that we do through Your Brilliance Unlimited. We have had phone calls and meetings everywhere from Thailand to France and have yet to be in the same room for any of them. Thank you for early morning text messages and for being so genuinely brilliant. Heather Bourque has gone above and beyond to help me when I needed insight and spark for design and forward ideas. We have traveled together in many bizarre places and always, there has been laughter and tears. Thanks!

Ashley Smart has been my tech guy, one of my closest friends and brother in so many ways for over 15 years. You have given me more insight than you will ever know and your wisdom has come at just the right time for bouncing ideas around about business and marketing. You are a gift to all who know you.

I live between two very different worlds and in both those places are people whom I love, respect and rely upon. To all of you in my worlds that have encouraged me and cheered on this project, thank you. You have made this journey one of much laughter and hope. Thanks for loving Widlene and me as your own and making us feel like we belong. Everyone deserves to feel that way in the worlds that they occupy and there are many people in both worlds that provide that for us.

Mom and Dad, I will forever be proud that in His infinite wisdom, God chose you for me. You make me want to be a better daughter and parent. You have proven to me and the world around you that there is hope after loss and there is always, always something to smile about and something new to learn. I love you and want to be like you when I grow up.

Augusto, your unfailing faith in me has been instrumental in healing a broken heart. Love is patient and kind and not self seeking. Your love is that for me. I hope I can be the same for you - always.

And finally, to the little tornado who came into my world and turned it upside down so that I could be right-side up: I love you, Widlene. Every day I am amazed that out of everyone on earth, you choose to call me Mom. Our journey has been marked by deep loss, but it has also been forever marked with deep love. You came when we all needed you, your love and laughter has healed our hearts, and your dreams are our vision for the future. Is there any greater gift in this life? I think not. Thank you for letting us love you.

About the Author

Christal Earle is a professional speaker, writer and coach, and the founder of Your Brilliance Unlimited. Previous to her current work, she was the co-founder and spokesperson for the Canadian-based charity, Live Different. She currently lives between Cabarete, Dominican Republic and Toronto, Ontario as she works to accomplish her greatest dream: bringing her daughter to Canada.

Printed in Canada